CATHOLICITY AND SECESSION

Catholicity and Secession

*A Study of Ecumenicity in the
Christian Reformed Church*

Henry Zwaanstra

William B. Eerdmans Publishing Company
Grand Rapids, Michigan

Copyright © 1991 by Wm. B. Eerdmans Publishing Co.
255 Jefferson Ave. S.E., Grand Rapids, Mich. 49503

A briefer exposition of the views in this book appears as a
chapter in *Catholicity and Secession: A Dilemma?*, edited
by Paul G. Schrotenboer (Kampen: J. H. Kok, 1991).

Printed in the United States of America

ISBN 0-8028-0604-X

for my daughter Kerrie Sue

Contents

Foreword

How does a conservative Protestant church deal with the problem of its separate existence as one denomination among many and the clear call of its Lord to manifest visibly to the world the unity of the body of Christ?

Denominationalism rests largely on the premise that loyalty to the truth takes precedence over the unity of the church because the unity of the church is rooted in and shaped by the truth. Preserving the truth is thus considered more important than the unity of the church.

In the twentieth century, however, two things have become increasingly clear. First, the unity of the church is itself a fundamental truth of the gospel which calls Christians to obedience in seeking visible expression of that unity. Loyalty to the truth includes commitment to the catholicity of the church. Secondly, the truth of the Christian faith is always mediated through and proclaimed by human beings who are fallible and imperfect in their perception of the truth so that no church can claim a final priority for its interpretation of the gospel. It is in ecumenical dialogue that we obtain a deeper common grasp of the truth.

An urgency exists in many denominations to address the tension between their separatism and their ecumenical responsibility. This book is a study of one denomination's struggle with its secession history and existence and its confession of the catholicity of the church. It may serve as a model of the dilemma that all conservative churches are facing.

This book is therefore deserving of a much larger readership than the members of the Christian Reformed Church. Many churches will recognize the parallelism between the Christian Reformed Church and their own denomination. They will identify with the problems of maintaining relations with other churches, of fostering church unions, and of being participants in ecumenical organizations.

As a competent church historian who has been active in his denomination's interchurch and ecumenical relations, Professor Henry Zwaanstra deals with an issue of fundamental concern for every church that seeks to be true to the gospel. It is a particularly timely subject for all churches in a world that is becoming increasingly united in its intolerance of the Christian faith and the influence of the church in our society.

Clarence Boomsma
Administrative Secretary of the
Interchurch Relations Committee of the
Christian Reformed Church in North America

Introduction

The Christian Reformed Church in North America (CRC) is biblically and creedally bound to confess the one holy catholic church of its Lord Jesus Christ. It is also scripturally and confessionally obligated to join and promote the unity of the holy congregation of believers in Christ and to separate from what is not the church — that is, the world and unbelief (Belgic Confession Art. 28). Consistent with its roots in the Protestant Reformation, the church has never divorced truth from unity. Catholicity for the sake of unity and separation for the sake of truth are the poles between which the church has historically attempted to navigate. Efforts to remove the poles and thus the tension between them by joining truth and unity have thus far for the most part eluded the church. The church has not yet been able to establish a satisfactory balance between unity and truth, either in its own consciousness or in its actual life. It remains neither comfortable in catholicity nor confident in separation and isolation. Historically the scales have tilted to the side of truth and separation, catholicity and unity being either neglected or implicitly denied. When the two have appeared to be in conflict, the church has rather consistently chosen for separation and what it perceived to be the truth.

The history of catholicity and secession in the CRC may conveniently be divided into four periods. The first three are each approximately forty years in length; the last just began with the adoption of the new Ecumenical Charter in 1987. The first period began with the Secession of 1834 in the Netherlands, and more particularly in America with the Secession of 1857. During this period a decidedly secessionist mentality dominated the life and thought of the church. The second period commenced in 1898 and continued until 1944. During this period a catholic Christian consciousness asserted itself within the church. The ecumenical activities of the church in this period were, however, strictly limited to official correspondence with other foreign and American Reformed churches, primarily for the purpose of maintaining purity in Reformed doctrine and practice. A third period began in 1944.[1] In this period the catholic consciousness and ecumenical vision of the church broadened and expanded to embrace all Christian churches. In its ecumenical activities, however, the CRC continued to restrict itself to full participation only within the narrow boundaries of Reformed confessional orthodoxy. A fourth period may have begun with the adoption of the Ecumenical Charter in 1987. The new charter continues to affirm an ecumenical calling to all churches of Christ. Without detracting from the importance of truth, it endorses CRC membership in ecumenical organizations that are not strictly confessional Reformed. The propriety of dialogue as a legitimate means to engage other churches in ecumenical conversation and as a method through which the church can learn as well as teach is a new feature of the charter. Whether or not the adoption of the charter will produce a new era of catholicity in the life of the CRC remains to be seen.

1. For a more equal distribution of the subject matter, this period is divided into two sections of approximately twenty years each: 1944–66 and 1966–87.

Secessionist Beginnings

The Secession of 1834

The CRC was born of two nineteenth-century secessions occurring in the short space of twenty-three years. The first secession was in 1834 from the Netherlands Reformed Church (NHK), the state church. This secession was part of an extensive spiritual and evangelical revival sweeping Western Europe in the wake of the Enlightenment and French Revolution of the previous century. The Christian secessionists protested the blatant rationalism and Liberalism in the NHK and vigorously objected to the reorganization of the churches introduced in 1816. In that year the Dutch churches were placed administratively under a government bureau of ecclesiastical affairs subject to the authority of the king. In the judgment of these secessionists the reorganized church clearly exhibited the marks of the false church, not the least of which was that it persecuted the true church. In conformity with Article 28 of the Belgic Confession they issued a call to all true believers to separate from the false church and to join the true church, the congregations of the Christian secessionists.

In 1840 in Amsterdam, the secessionists officially organized a church on the ecclesiastical foundations of the Reformed churches in the Netherlands in the sixteenth and early seventeenth centuries. The Belgic Confession, the Heidelberg Catechism, and the Canons of the Synod of Dort

1

(1618–19) were accepted as the confessional standards of the church; its life was to be regulated by the church order adopted at Dort. Because the secessionists believed all the articles of faith and doctrines contained in these standards fully agreed with God's Word, strict subscription to them was required by officeholders. In keeping with the highest traditions of the Reformed fathers, the Reformed standards and the church order were to be scrupulously applied to the life of the church. Neither the secession nor the newly organized church were intended to introduce and secure some new, radical idea, as has often been true of separatist movements. Their purpose was rather to return to and defend the historical Reformed position from which the NHK had departed.

The seceders were rewarded for their courage and conviction with the heavy and oppressive hand of official persecution. During the following decade their plight was rendered more intolerable by economic depression, a burden to some extent borne by all, but especially by the secessionists. In order to secure better living conditions for themselves and their posterity and in order to worship God freely and unhindered in submission to his Word, a group of these Reformed seceders decided to make a new beginning in America. Under the leadership of Rev. Albertus C. Van Raalte they started a colony at Holland in western Michigan early in 1847. Other emigrants soon followed. Already in 1848 Dutch immigrant churches had organized a classis, Classis Holland.

The Secession of 1857

The second secession occurred in 1857, following a union of the churches of Classis Holland with the Reformed Church in America (RCA).[1] In both the union and the later

1. The official name of the church at the time was Reformed

separation fundamental issues regarding the catholicity of the church and the right to secede inevitably surfaced and were debated.

In 1849 the Board of Domestic Missions of the RCA commissioned Dr. I. N. Wyckoff to visit the Dutch immigrant churches in western Michigan. The purpose of his visit undoubtedly was to explore with them the possibility of church union. After a severe winter, Wyckoff found the Dutch pioneers weak, impoverished, and not a little demoralized. A classical meeting was hastily called. Unfortunately no minutes were recorded. Wyckoff's report to the board indicates that the colonists were afraid of a union with the church in the East. To allay their fears, Wyckoff told them that they would be most perfectly free, at any time they found the union opposed to their religious prosperity or enjoyment, to bid a fraternal adieu and again be by themselves.[2] With this conditional promise a decision evidently was made to join the RCA.

In April 1850 Classis Holland sent a letter, written by Van Raalte, to the particular synod of the RCA meeting in Albany, New York. Paraphrasing Scripture, the letter breathed a genuinely catholic spirit.

> In consideration of the precious and blessed unity of the church of God, and the clearly declared will of our Saviour that they all should be one; as well as the need which the particular parts of the whole have of one another —

Protestant Dutch Church. The name was changed in 1867 to the Reformed Church in America. The primary source for the union and secession is *Minutes of Classis Holland 1848–1858*, trans. by a joint committee of the CRC and the RCA (Grand Rapids: Wm. B. Eerdmans, 1950).

2. Report, Board of Domestic Missions, 1850. Quoted from Henry Beets, *De Chr. Geref. Kerk in N.A.* (Grand Rapids: Grand Rapids Printing Co., 1918), p. 102. Beets argued that the union between the churches of Classis Holland and the RCA was illegal because those present at the meeting were not delegated by their consistories. He also viewed the action of those separating from the RCA as a legitimate return to the circumstances present in 1849, and not as a secession, because of the conditional nature of the joining. See Beets, pp. 70-72, 102.

especially we, who feel our weakness and insignificance —
our hearts thirst for fellowship with the beloved Zion of God.

Since the day that we stepped ashore in this new world,
our hearts have been strengthened and encouraged by
meeting the people of God. The children of God are all dear
to us, living in their respective denominations, but in guiding and caring for the interests of our congregations we find
ourselves best at home where we are privileged to find our
own confessional standards and the fundamental principles
of our church government. Thus it was gratifying to us to
experience from the other side [RCA] no narrow exclusive-
ness, but open hearty, brotherly love. This awakens in us a
definite desire to make manifest our fellowship, and to ask
for the hand of brotherly fellowship in return.[3]

In May the particular synod of Albany acted favorably on
Classis Holland's request. The following month at the
general synod of Poughkeepsie the churches of Classis Holland were accepted into the fellowship of the RCA.

Almost from the beginning — with ever-increasing
frequency and over a widening range of issues and concerns
— voices were heard expressing serious doubts about the
wisdom and propriety of the Union of 1850. At the September 1855 meeting of classis, Rev. C. Vander Meulen and
elder J. Vande Luister reported on the meetings of the
recent synod held in New Brunswick, New Jersey. The
synodical delegates judged that the RCA confessionally was
in complete agreement with the Reformed fathers. They
had, however, discovered some deficiency in regular catechism preaching and laxity in church discipline. At the
classical meeting it was not the doctrines held and taught,
but the practices of the RCA that were subjected to critical
review and comment.

The celebration of the Lord's Supper — the sacrament
of Christian unity — became the focal point of the most
heated debate and the sharpest dissent. Gysbert Haan, a

---

3. *Minutes of Classis Holland,* pp. 36-37.

delegate from Grand Rapids, asked what happened at the synod in regard to the synodical celebration of the Lord's Supper. Vander Meulen answered that the synod faced the problem of whether or not to restrict the privilege of participation to the delegates alone, thus excluding all others present. The synod had decided to invite the professors and students of New Brunswick Seminary, the president, professors, and pious students of Rutgers College, and the other Christians from the city who were present, regardless of their denominational affiliation, to unite with it in Holy Communion. Vander Meulen further informed the assembly that it was the custom among the orthodox churches in America to admit members of other Christian churches to the table of the Lord. A lively discussion ensued. A delegate read Article 28 of the Belgic Confession, which states that believers are obliged to unite with the church and to separate from that which is not the church. He then asked whether or not, still today, Reformed churches should only recognize other Reformed churches as true churches. He also asked whether or not the Lord's Supper, when administered in a Reformed church, should be served only to members of the congregation and those of other Reformed churches, excluding converted people from other denominations. Much was said pro and con. The classis postponed action on the matter until the next meeting.

Rev. H. G. Klyn, a minister from Grand Rapids, was not present at the September 1855 classis meeting. He did, however, send a letter explaining why he had not attended the general synod even though he had been a delegate. The letter contained an admonition and exhortation to classis to insist that persons who enter the ministry should have no doubt in their hearts that the Reformed confessions are "the standard of the faith and the only way of salvation."

At the April 1856 meeting of classis, Haan, relying on a New Brunswick student's report, charged that the synod of the RCA had adopted a resolution to admit members of all denominations to the Lord's Supper. Again Vander

Meulen and Vande Luister insisted that no such resolution had been adopted or even brought up for discussion. The only question that had been discussed was whether or not people from orthodox churches present at the synodical communion service should be invited to partake. Van Raalte said that members of American denominations living in the same place do not indiscriminately mix together for the celebration of the Lord's Supper, but it was true that visitors and those passing through were sometimes invited to take part in the celebration even though they were members of another denomination.

In the course of the debate Haan was accused of schismatic activity. Haan's response was that although he was opposed to secession, he had always doubted that the RCA was the true church, a judgment based on the unfavorable things he had heard about it.

A year later, in April 1857, Classis Holland was confronted with four letters of withdrawal and separation. These letters differed in style and tone; in content they were essentially the same. The Rev. Koene Vanden Bosch, a recent arrival from the Netherlands, sent a brief, caustic letter to the Zeeland consistory, simply stating that he could no longer be in ecclesiastical fellowship with the Zeeland church because he did not believe that the congregations which had joined the RCA were the true church of Jesus Christ. He further stated that he was constrained to renounce all fellowship with the church out of fear of God and on account of the abominable church-destroying heresy and sin rampant in the RCA. Vanden Bosch promised to present a statement of the heresies and sins to the next meeting of classis, but he did not keep his promise.

Rev. Klyn's letter was considerably more affectionate. In addition to announcing his withdrawal from the American denomination, he reminded the brethren — especially the ministers — that they had stood together and together walked the same path in the Netherlands. There they had been separate from all other Protestant denominations. He concluded with an exhortation not to lose their separatist character, "for the church, the Bride of Christ, is a garden enclosed, a well shut up, and a fountain sealed."

The letter of the Polkton consistory informed the classis that the church no longer belonged to the RCA. It was again assuming the standpoint it had when leaving the Netherlands. The consistory gave one reason for its action: the denomination which the classis had joined fraternized with those who opposed the doctrinal teaching of the Reformed fathers.

The Graafschaap consistory submitted the most elaborate statement of secession. In its statement the consistory informed the classis of its present ecclesiastical standpoint, further describing it as separation not only from the RCA, but from all Protestant denominations with which the Dutch immigrant churches thoughtlessly became connected upon their arrival in America. At the same time the consistory informed the classis that it was uniting with the secession churches in the Netherlands and affectionately exhorted the churches of the classis to do the same. Six reasons, for the most part touching practices in the RCA, were given for the Graafschaap church's decision.[4] The letter concluded by saying: "We . . . again stand upon the same standpoint on which our fathers enjoyed so great

4. 1) Using a collection of 800 hymns introduced contrary to the church order; 2) inviting people of all religious views to the Lord's Supper, excepting Roman Catholics; 3) neglecting to preach the catechism regularly, to hold catechetical classes, and to do home visitation; 4) refusing to circulate religious books without the consent of other denominations (it was mistakenly assumed that the RCA was party to an agreement not to circulate or use in the Sunday schools any books unless they had been approved by fourteen denominations); 5) what grieves our hearts most in all this is that there are members among you who regard our secession in the Netherlands as not strictly necessary or think that it was untimely; and 6) in his report Rev. Wyckoff gives us liberty to walk in this ecclesiastical path. *Minutes of Classis Holland*, p. 242. The presence of Freemasons in the RCA was not mentioned in the consistory's letter, but the minutes of a Graafschaap congregational meeting held February 4, 1857, indicate that this too was a matter of concern. See Beets, pp. 92-93.

blessedness, and oh, we should rejoice still more if the King of the church should bring you to this conviction. This is the duty of us all. The God of love be your counsellor and guide you to walk in the way of love."[5]

The secessionists of 1857 were evidently serious about joining the church in the Netherlands. The same month Klyn and Vanden Bosch sent a letter to the synod of the church there, requesting recognition as a part of the church in the Netherlands. The letter was read at the synod, but no specific action was taken on the request and, consequently, no official recognition was granted. Early in May 1857 the four seceding churches — Graafschaap, Grand Rapids, Polkton, and Noordeloos — organized a classis on the same basis as that of the church in the Netherlands: God's Word, according to the Reformed confessional standards and the Church Order of Dort.

In the secessions of 1834 and 1857, catholicity and the unity of all believers in the one body of Christ suffered severe blows. The propriety, right, and necessity of secession and separation were affirmed virtually without qualification. No real distinctions were made between essential and nonessential or less essential matters in a church's doctrine, polity, and life. Most crucial for understanding the seceders' thought and action was the meaning of "our standpoint." The specific content of this term was God's Word, set forth doctrinally in the confessional standards of the historic Reformed church in the Netherlands and structurally in the church order adopted at the Synod of Dort. Where this doctrine was taught and maintained and where this polity was consistently and vigorously practiced, the secessionists were confident the true church of Christ was present. Where, however, there was any deviation from this position or standpoint in doctrine, polity, and practice, they tended to doubt the real presence of Christ's church. The secessionists had struggled and suffered for this ecclesiastical

5. *Minutes of Classis Holland*, p. 242.

position in the Netherlands. Now in America they feared it had been surrendered or at least seriously compromised in the Union of 1850. In order to return to and secure it for posterity, they thought they had to sever relationships with the RCA and all other Protestant denominations in America. Only by separation and return could they be confident that they stood within the unity of the true church, which for all practical purposes to them was synonymous with the historic Reformed church of the Netherlands. In their judgment this church had been reborn in the recent secessions.

The secessions of 1834 and 1857 — especially the latter — had a profound formative influence on the CRC. They contributed to the formation of a deep and sharply delimited confessional Reformed self-consciousness and sense of identity. They stimulated interest in the study of Reformed doctrine and engendered intense denominational loyalty. There were also, however, less favorable consequences. The secessions produced a staunchly conservative, traditional, rigid, and unimaginative mentality. Separation and the defense of it nurtured parochialism, elitism, and social cohesiveness. Attitudes of superiority and, at times, smugness and blatant arrogance came to characterize the secessionists and their descendants in matters pertaining to the church and theology. Social and ecclesiastical isolation, buttressed by ethnicity, produced an exclusivist mentality and a negatively critical attitude, often tinged with suspicion, toward the American churches. The unity of all believers in Christ and the importance of bringing that unity to visible expression eluded the secessionists as they expended their energies in forming a purer and more Reformed church.

Early in its history the CRC did not flourish. Internal conflicts and unfruitful controversies sapped the church's vitality. Some ministers, after a brief period of service, defected to the RCA.[6] Disappointment and discourage-

6. Rev. Klyn, for example, who seceded in April, returned to the RCA in September.

ment were so intense that in 1863 one of the congregations proposed disbanding and joining the Old School Presbyterian Church. Two ministers from the Scottish Presbyterian Church, who no doubt were aware that this matter was on the agenda of classis, were present at the meeting. They voluntarily reported for the classis' benefit the serious defects in the Old School church. They also encouraged the delegates to join their church. After considerable discussion, Rev. Vanden Bosch reminded the classis that it had recently assumed the title "True Dutch Reformed Church."[7] He no doubt further explained the obvious implications of the title. An elder delegate then spoke about the purity of the church's standpoint and warned against "hankering after the flesh-pots of Egypt." The classis decided not to join either of the Presbyterian bodies.[8]

Conditions improved significantly for the CRC after 1880.[9] Several factors contributed to increased strength and prosperity. As a result of the Freemasonry controversy in the RCA, a few churches and a substantial number of members seceded from the Reformed Church and joined the CRC. Since the churches in the Netherlands were strenuously opposed to the Freemasons, they now began to advise members emigrating to America to join the CRC rather than the RCA because the CRC repudiated membership in all oath-bound societies. After 1880 the CRC benefited from

---

7. Two years after the Secession of 1857, the name "Dutch Reformed Church" was officially adopted. Probably for polemical reasons, the name was changed to the "True Dutch Reformed Church" in 1861. In 1880 the name was again changed to "Holland Christian Reformed Church," a name conforming with the name assumed in 1869 by the secessionist churches in the Netherlands, "De Christelijke Gereformeerde Kerk." Ten years later, as a concession to the English-speaking churches of the True Reformed Dutch Church, "Holland" was dropped from the church's official name.

8. The primary source for this early history is *Notulen van de Classicale Vergadering der Hollandse Gereformeerde Kerk in America,* 1857–1865.

9. The churches first met as a synod in 1880.

the rapidly increasing number of emigrants from the Netherlands.

Church Union Movements

In 1890 the CRC united with the True Reformed Dutch Church, a church that had seceded from the RCA in 1822. The only instance of organic union with another denomination in the history of the CRC, this merger was not motivated by the scriptural and confessional ideals of the catholicity and unity of the church. A common history of secession from the RCA and complete unanimity in confessional standards and doctrine provided the basis for the merger, in spite of the fact that the congregations of the True Reformed Dutch Church were English-speaking. (Dutch was, with the exception of one congregation, still the language of the CRC.) The ten congregations of the True Reformed Church were obviously in a state of decline when they, by a small majority, voted to seek union with the CRC rather than dissolve their church fellowship. Their decision to unite with the CRC included certain conditions and contingencies. The True Reformed Church insisted on maintaining its own internal government and patterns of public worship. The congregations of the True Reformed Church were organized as a separate CRC classis, Classis Hackensack, and were permitted to use a limited number of hymns in public worship.

Unfortunately, the union was not satisfying or happy for either party. Linguistic and ethnic differences presented difficulties. By entering the CRC as a separate classis with its own internal government, the congregations of the True Reformed Church never became an integral part of the CRC, and consequently a genuinely organic merger never occurred. The churches of Classis Hackensack were from the beginning harassed by the Dutch churches. The Dutch

11

churches, in turn, were deeply distressed by the presence of lodge members in the churches of Classis Hackensack and by the fact that the English-speaking churches expanded their collection of hymns from the original fifty-two approved by the synod to one hundred and ninety. In 1908 all except three of the churches of Classis Hackensack decided to dissolve the union.

In 1888, at the initiative of the United Presbyterian Church of North America (UPC),[10] the CRC became involved in interchurch-relation discussions lasting almost a decade. Striking similarities in the history, doctrinal position, and church life of the two denominations as well as mutual advantages for their life and ministry made closer relations between the churches seem attractive.

The Presbyterians originally proposed and continued to press for organic union. The CRC and its representatives, however, never seriously considered organic or corporate union a real option. Hendricus Beuker, spokesman for the CRC in the conversations, contended that the CRC and the UPC, although one in the fundamentally important matters of doctrine, government, and church life, were sufficiently different in the relatively important matters of national origin, history, and language to disallow an organic union. Beuker and the CRC expressed a preference for a cooperative union, more like a sister-church relationship, in which the two churches would mutually recognize each other as churches and cooperate in ministry and church programs. When it became increasingly apparent that organic union was the only kind of union in which the UPC was interested, the CRC lost interest. Because of the differences in size, a union of the two denominations, it was assumed, would amount to no less than the absorption of the CRC into the

10. The United Presbyterian Church was formed as a result of a merger of the Associate Presbyterian Church and the Associate Reformed Presbyterian Church at Pittsburgh in 1858. A hundred years later, in 1958, this church joined the Presbyterian Church in the U.S.A. to form the United Presbyterian Church in the U.S.A.

UPC. The loss of its distinctively Dutch Reformed confessional and ecclesiastical heritage — and even its name — was a price the CRC was unwilling either to pay or to wager for the cause of church union.

Ethnic considerations also influenced the thinking of the church. If the two denominations merged, Reformed emigrants from the Netherlands very likely would not join the united church. Consequently, they would find themselves without an acceptable church home in America. Leaders in the CRC, even participants in the discussions, did not conceal the fact that they much preferred an organic union with their kinsmen in the RCA rather than with an American Presbyterian denomination. In 1898 the synod decided to terminate the conversations. The mind of the CRC was clear. Maintaining its ethnic and distinctively Reformed identity was more important than the church unity that could be achieved by merging with a larger American Presbyterian church.[11]

The church-union discussions in the Netherlands between the churches of the Secession of 1834 and the Doleantie (a secession movement from the NHK under the leadership of Dr. Abraham Kuyper in 1886) were watched with considerable interest by the Dutch immigrant churches in America. When the Reformed Churches in the Netherlands (GKN) were formed in 1892, the union was greeted in America with enthusiasm, stimulating new interest in church union among the Dutch immigrant churches there. A lively discussion followed in the Dutch church papers, permeated with references and appeals to a common ethnic and ecclesiastical heritage and filled with expressions of regret that the churches were separated when they really belonged together. Unofficial committees composed of rep-

11. The primary sources for synodical decisions are: *Synodale Handelingen der Hollandsche Christelijke Gereformeerde Kerk in Amerika*, 1880–92; *Acta van de Synode der Christelijke Gereformeerde Kerk in Amerika*, 1894–1926; *Acta der Synode van de Christelijke Gereformeerde Kerk*, 1928-30; and *Acts of the Synod of the Christian Reformed Church*, 1930–88.

resentatives of both churches were formed, programs for union and cooperation were drawn up by the respective committees, and a public meeting or conference to discuss the proposed plans was scheduled for November 1894, in the historic Van Raalte church in Holland, Michigan. It soon became apparent, however, that the issues were joined in such a way that the churches could not be joined.

The Reformed church representatives in their program first observed that the Reformed and Christian Reformed churches were one in confession, church government, and the principles concerning church life. They then stated their profound conviction that the historical RCA was the true and proper home for the Dutch Reformed people in America. They further declared that they would not consider discussing any union that contained the prospect of possible withdrawal from the RCA, and that, in their judgment, there was no substantial ground or reason for the CRC to remain separate from the RCA.

The Christian Reformed representatives in their program expressed regret that those holding the same confessions and desiring to live according to the same church order were still ecclesiastically separated. They pointed out the disadvantages of the present separation with regard to the influence of the churches in the world, the education of the youth, and the spiritual life of the congregations. After referring to the necessity of applying the Reformed confessions to life and of exercising church discipline, the program they formulated unequivocally declared membership in all oath-bound secret societies incompatible with church membership. The CRC was obviously interested in union only with the Western or Dutch-speaking branch of the RCA, consisting of those immigrant churches that had entered the RCA in 1850 and had not seceded in 1857. The CRC felt the common bonds of language, nationality, and ecclesiastical origin with these churches.

These common bonds, however, were not strong enough to bring the Dutch immigrant congregations in the

14

RCA to break unity with the churches in the East, or even seriously to discuss dissolving the union entered into in 1850. Nor were the bonds strong enough to induce the CRC to surrender its separate identity and understanding of what it meant to be a genuinely and consistently Reformed church in practice as well as in doctrine.[12]

---

12. For more elaborate discussions of these early efforts for church union, see John H. Kromminga, *The Christian Reformed Church: A Study in Orthodoxy* (Grand Rapids: Baker Book House, 1949), pp. 104-11; and Henry Zwaanstra, *A Study of the Christian Reformed Church and its American Environment 1890–1918* (Kampen: J. H. Kok, 1973), pp. 9-23.

Catholicity Affirmed

Church Correspondence

Prior to 1898 the CRC corresponded on an irregular basis with the Evangelical Church in Silesia, the Old German Reformed Church in Prussia, the Christian Reformed Church in the Netherlands, and the Reformed Church in South Africa (RCSA). The South African church, consisting for the most part of nineteenth-century Dutch emigrants who seceded from the older and larger Dutch Reformed Church (DRC), was very much like the CRC in history, doctrine, and life.

In 1898 the synod of the CRC noted that in recent years Reformed churches had done very little in the area of official church correspondence. This was in striking contrast to the flourishing period in the life of the Reformed churches in the sixteenth and seventeenth centuries, when sister churches engaged in fellowship and mutual admonition in order to purge themselves of all non-Reformed elements. The rise of collegialism in church government and of denominationalism, it was presumed, contributed to the demise of the earlier practice. Official church correspondence was required by God's Word, which clearly teaches that churches need one another. Now, in agreement with the New Testament vision of the world church, the synod said, the old doctrine of the catholicity of the church was beginning to live again. Church correspondence therefore must be revived and more carefully regulated.

Official correspondence, the synod said, should not be reduced to exchanging fraternal delegates and expressing cordial greetings at major assemblies, but should consist of the following:

a) sending delegates to each other's major assemblies with an advisory vote;
b) fraternal admonitions to each other lest any church depart from Reformed principles in doctrine, worship, or polity;
c) discussion with each other regarding relationships with third parties;
d) giving each other advice, particularly in the discussion of changes in confession, church order, and liturgy.

The synod expressed the wish that this kind of well-circumscribed correspondence with sister churches in the Reformed family might soon come into existence. In keeping with its newly aroused sense of catholicity, the synod said it would rejoice if before long a general synod or council of Reformed churches could assemble for the twofold purpose of assisting churches to purify themselves of all foreign or non-Reformed elements and of helping one another to promote a soundly Reformed church life. Only if a synod or council of this kind and with this purpose came into existence could complete unity and a well-ordered system of correspondence between all Reformed churches be realized.

For the time being the synod decided to attempt to establish correspondence with the Reformed Churches in the Netherlands, the Old Reformed Church in Germany, the Reformed Church in South Africa, the United Presbyterian Church in North America, and the Reformed Church in America — particularly its Dutch branch.

A committee on church correspondence was appointed to implement the synod's program and vision. Another committee was appointed to investigate the Presbyterian churches in America and Scotland to determine if and how far correspondence with some of them might be possible. Correspondence with these churches, the synod carefully pointed out, naturally did not mean that they should be viewed as in every respect in agreement with the CRC in confession, church order, and practice. They were, after all, historically Presbyterian and not Reformed.

The CRC's awakened interest in catholicity and these decisions regarding church correspondence were probably occasioned in no small measure by the fact that the Alliance of Reformed Churches holding the Presbyterian system of government that year invited the synod to become a member of the alliance. A study committee was appointed to investigate the matter and to report to the next synod. Upon the recommendation of the committee, the Synod of 1900 decided not yet to enter the alliance because membership in the alliance seemed to be determined more by a commitment to the Presbyterian system of church government than by a definite commitment to the Reformed confessions. For example, the Cumberland Presbyterian Church, a church holding Arminian doctrine, was a member. The synod also judged that the alliance as presently constituted could not be what the CRC, for reasons of Reformed principle, desired. The church really wanted a worldwide synod of definitely Calvinistic churches united for the purpose of strengthening their Reformed confessional position.

Upon the recommendation of the committee appointed to investigate other Presbyterian churches with a view to possible correspondence, the synod in 1900 decided to extend the privilege of correspondence to the Reformed Presbyterian Church in North America (Covenanters), the General Synod in the Reformed Presbyterian Church, and the Associate Presbyterian Church, in addition to the previously approved United Presbyterian Church. In the judgment of the synod all four of these churches "stood with both feet on the Westminster Confession," preached the full council of God, and opposed secret oath-bound societies, the "cancer of modern-day church life." The synod decided not to enter a relationship of correspondence with the Presbyterian Church in the U.S. (Southern) or with the Associate Reformed Presbyterian Church because these churches, although sound in doctrine, had not yet taken a stand against oath-bound societies. Since elements of the newer theology had crept into and were tolerated in the Free Church of Scotland and the Presbyterian Church in the U.S.A., the synod decided not to correspond with them, but "to watch them."

The standards for official correspondence presented difficulties in establishing a relationship with the American church with which the CRC was historically and confessionally the most closely related. Recognizing the problem, the Synod of 1900 sent a delegation to discuss with the general synod of the RCA the recently adopted terms and conditions for correspondence. The delegation was also specifically commissioned (1) to request the general synod to review its position on secret oath-bound societies and to decide whether or not to oppose them, and (2) to express the wish that the RCA would restore as a part of its confessional standards the Rejection of Errors in the Canons of Dort.[1]

The RCA did not comply with either of the CRC's requests. It also refused correspondence on the CRC's terms. The Reformed Church did, however, offer to continue fraternal relationships with the CRC on the same conditions and with the same understanding as with other churches. While regretting that the RCA had so little understanding of the solidarity of the Reformed churches and of official church correspondence in the Reformed sense, the CRC decided to continue correspondence with the RCA.

---

1. The general synod of the RCA deleted the sections of the Canons rejecting the errors of the Remonstrants in 1792, because of their negative character and irrelevance to the contemporary American scene.

The ideal of church correspondence was at best only partially realized. Correspondence was carried on with the GKN, including periodic exchange of fraternal delegates. With the RCSA even less frequent correspondence, always by letter, was continued. Distances between the churches, however, rendered mutual consultation virtually impossible.

More frequent exchange of fraternal delegates took place between the CRC and the American corresponding churches; but these exchanges, amounting to little more than an exchange of cordial greetings, never attained the ideals and goals originally envisioned. During the Great Depression even this practice fell into general disuse.

The synod in 1940 was not pleased with the current status of church correspondence. Especially troubling for the synod was the fact that for no apparent reason some churches were classified as sister churches and others as churches in correspondence. The synod was also concerned about how little was known regarding the actual state of affairs in and practices of some of the churches with which the CRC had a relationship of official correspondence. Moreover, it seemed to the synod that there were probably other Reformed churches with which the CRC should have a formal relationship. The synod, therefore, decided not to resume correspondence with churches with which it had lapsed, nor to admit any churches to an official status until the basis and standards for such recognition were carefully defined.[2] The committee on church correspondence was asked to undertake a special study including the following:

2. At the time the synod had on its agenda a proposal to recognize the Orthodox Presbyterian Church (OPC) as a sister church. This church, which had seceded from the Presbyterian Church in the U.S.A. in 1936 as a result of the Fundamentalist-modernist controversy, had much in common with the CRC. The CRC was not, however, ready to grant the OPC the intimacy of a sister-church relationship because the OPC had not yet taken a stand against lodges and did not require members to subscribe to a Reformed confession.

a. To make a careful study of the basis, the aim, the scope, and the norms, for the practice of correspondence with other churches, and to make definite proposals for adoption regarding these matters.

b. To make a study of the creedal position, the doctrinal attitude, the conditions for membership and the practice of church discipline prevailing in such bodies of the historic Reformed tradition which might come into consideration (both at home and abroad) for correspondence with our church.

c. . . . to make a study of past decisions of synod anent correspondence with other churches.

d. To propose, in the light of this study, a revised list of churches with which our church should stand in the relation of official correspondence, grouping them, and specifying how in the case of each group the actual correspondence may be made most effective and fruitful.[3]

The committee had a big assignment. It reported nothing in 1941. The following year it again reported nothing. In 1943 the committee reported that it had been inactive due to Dr. Henry Beets' resignation as stated clerk and Rev. John Dolfin's illness. The synod that year decided to merge the committee previously assigned to work toward the organization of a Reformed ecumenical council and the committee for church correspondence, thus substantially increasing the scope of the committee's work.

Membership in the Federal Council of Christian Churches

The decision of the CRC to become a member of the Federal Council of Christian Churches (FCCC) in 1918 did not arise out of a deepening ecumenical consciousness or a clearer

3. *Acts of Synod, 1940*, p. 68.

21

understanding of the implications of the catholicity of the church. Rather, the CRC wanted chaplains to minister to its men in military service. During World War I the United States government classified all denominations that were not members of the FCCC as miscellaneous churches. Very few positions in the military chaplaincy were open to churches so classified. The Red Cross, which also called and placed military chaplains, worked exclusively through the FCCC. The CRC, therefore, without previous study or serious reflection, hastily joined the council in order to acquire a more acceptable official standing among the American churches for the purpose of placing military chaplains.

Immediately after the war the synod was confronted with requests to terminate this membership. A committee, consisting of the Revs. John Dolfin and John Timmerman, was appointed to review and evaluate arguments given both for and against membership in the FCCC. In their report to the following synod, Dolfin and Timmerman first observed that the CRC joined the FCCC at its own initiative. After answering standing objections, the two acknowledged that anyone looking for flaws in the Federal Council could find them. Finally, the study committee gave its position and advice. The CRC's first aim, they said, should not be to receive benefits from but to give of itself to the American churches. It should serve the churches by exerting an influence for good and by constantly presenting within the FCCC its Reformed views. The denomination, the committee argued, should surely be represented in a body that speaks for a united American Protestantism and, by the nature of the case, for the CRC. The committee also anticipated that in the future the church would need the support of the council in its missionary work and other activities. Dolfin and Timmerman therefore advised the synod not to withdraw but to appoint some of the church's most capable men to represent it in the council. The synod followed the committee's advice and delegated Dolfin, Timmerman, and Beets to the next meeting of the FCCC.

At the next synod in 1924, the delegates reported very positively on the breadth and quality of the national and international programs of the FCCC in the postwar reconstruction years. They also reported scoring some successes: Dolfin and Timmerman were appointed to the executive committee; Beets was made a vice president. Anticipating that the Federal Council would be criticized for its Liberalism, the three said that the addresses of the president, Dr. Robert E. Speer, and the chairman of the administrative committee, John M. Moore, had been very good and that it was unfair to hold the council responsible for all the utterances of its commissions and their spokesmen. The council should be held responsible only for official statements, and even these, it was noted, were not binding on any member denomination. Just as many CRC ministers were members of local ministerial conferences without assuming responsibility for all that these conferences said and did, so too the church as a member of an interdenominational conference should not consider itself responsible for all that was said and done by the various parties connected with the council.

Some Christian Reformed churches did not share the delegates' opinion and judgment. Requests were again presented to synod calling for termination of membership on the grounds that the FCCC was controlled by liberals and was decidedly liberal in its principles, even advocating humanistic religion and promoting the organization of the united church of the future. Opposition was also expressed to the council's industrial, national, and international programs that some thought did not belong to the province of the church. The opponents of continued membership argued that the CRC, simply by virtue of its membership, was jointly responsible for the propaganda and other statements of the council's commissions and spokesmen. They also strenuously objected to remaining in the organization because membership in it was not restricted to orthodox churches. Alliances of any kind between orthodox and liberals, they were convinced, were contrary to the Word of God.

The Synod of 1924 decided to sever all connections with the FCCC. A variety of factors and conditions both external and internal to the life of the CRC no doubt influenced the decision. The rapid advance of Liberalism in mainline American Protestant denominations, especially after World War I, was one factor. The CRC's own internal struggle with Liberalism in the Janssen case in 1922 was another.[4] The imminent threat of division within its own ranks posed by conservative elements under the leadership of the Revs. Herman Hoeksema and Henry Danhof, who denied common grace,[5] also no doubt contributed in some measure to the synod's decision. The alleged Liberalism of the Federal Council itself was, however, the overriding concern and reason for the synod's action.[6]

An Invitation to Discuss Church Union Declined

In 1930 the CRC was invited to participate with five other Presbyterian and Reformed churches in conversations aiming, if possible, at organic union. The five churches were the Presbyterian Church in the U.S.A., the Presbyterian Church in the U.S. (Southern), the Reformed Church in America, the Reformed Church in the U.S. (German Reformed), and the United Presbyterian Church of North

4. Dr. Roelof Janssen, professor of Old Testament at Calvin Theological Seminary, was deposed in 1922, allegedly for holding higher-critical views and undermining the supernatural character of divine revelation.

5. As a result of the synod's affirmation of common grace, Hoeksema and Danhof formed a new denomination, the Protestant Reformed Church.

6. For a more detailed history of the CRC and the FCCC, see John Kromminga, *The Christian Reformed Church*, pp. 111-15.

America. Although declining the invitation, the CRC availed itself of the opportunity to affirm its faith in the unity of the church of Christ, a unity which, though essentially spiritual, should come to visible expression in the organized church. It also expressed a desire to cultivate a spirit of mutual understanding and cooperation between Calvinistic churches.

The reasons given for not participating in the conversations present a striking contrast between the CRC's perception of its own doctrine and life and its perception of the teachings and practices of the other churches. The CRC, it was said, stood "foursquare" for the Reformed interpretation of Christian truth as expressed in its confessional standards and it could not consider organic union with church bodies in which there was widespread indifference toward the great essentials of the Reformed faith, as was the case in at least one of the cooperating bodies. (The reference was undoubtedly to the Presbyterian Church in the U.S.A.) In the struggle between modernism and orthodoxy raging in the historic Christian churches, the CRC was committed to the orthodox, biblical, and supernatural view of the Christian faith and could not consider organic union with churches that did not unequivocally affirm and maintain this position. In at least one of the participating denominations, modernism was not only tolerated but openly propagated in pulpit, press, and theological education.

The contrast was also evident in church discipline. The CRC maintained discipline in both doctrine and Christian living, while church discipline in some of the five cooperating churches had practically fallen into disuse. Specifically, the CRC judged membership in oath-bound secret societies incompatible with membership in the church. Organic union with the five churches, it was assumed, could be realized only at the expense of this prerequisite, a sacrifice the CRC was not prepared to make.

The Reformed Ecumenical Synod

At the same time that the CRC was drawing sharp lines of separation between itself as an orthodox Reformed body and all other liberal churches and church organizations, it was moving slowly yet steadily forward in its efforts to form a Reformed international synod. The vision of the Synod of 1898 for a worldwide, general council or synod of Reformed churches lay dormant until 1920. The synod of the CRC that year asked its fraternal delegate to the general synod of the GKN, Dr. Henry Beets, to inform the synod that, in the judgment of the CRC, synods of confessional Reformed churches of Dutch origin throughout the world should take into consideration in their deliberations and decision- making the opinion of the other Dutch Reformed churches. Such a practice was in keeping with the meaning and intention of official church correspondence. Beets' appointment as director of missions made it impossible for him to attend the general synod in the Netherlands. Instead he sent a letter saying that in these times of spiritual struggle Reformed churches needed each other's support and advice more than ever before. In order to demonstrate that the churches believe in the fellowship of the saints and still experience the solidarity of the Reformed churches worldwide, Beets proposed a continuing effort to form a general council of Reformed churches of Dutch origin. In 1924 Professor H. H. Kuyper, fraternal delegate from the GKN to the synod of the RCSA, presented the substance of Beets' proposal in a somewhat more specific and elaborate form to the church in South Africa. According to Kuyper the ideal to be pursued should be a Reformed ecumenical synod of all churches still firmly holding to the Reformed confessions, not one including churches that were just historically and officially Reformed. Beets' and Kuyper's proposal did not bear immediate fruit.

In 1930 the synod of the RCSA adopted a recommendation expressing a desire that an interdenominational Reformed synod or international Calvinistic congress be organized. This recommendation of the South African church was sent to the CRC and GKN. Two years later the synod of the CRC responded very positively to the idea, stating that a convention of delegates from all the Reformed churches was an ideal worthy of most serious thought and the most careful consideration. An assembly of this kind would constitute a highly desirable expression of the unity of Christ's church and would offer a splendid opportunity for discussing weighty problems of general interest that periodically arise in the Reformed churches. The synod nevertheless judged that the present time of economic depression was not propitious for calling such a convention. The synod did, however, appoint a committee to correspond on the matter with the churches in the Netherlands and South Africa.

Reformed ecumenical activity revived in 1938, when Dr. G. Ch. Aalders, representing the GKN's committee for correspondence with foreign churches, asked the CRC to express an opinion on four pertinent questions: Who should call together an eventual synod? Which churches should be invited? How was delegating to take place? And what should be put on the agenda of an eventual synod? The synod of the CRC concurred in the judgment of its committee for a Reformed ecumenical council that the GKN should call the synod for reasons of historical priority. All three of the churches that had thus far corresponded on the matter originated in the Netherlands, which was also the most centrally located and easiest spot to reach. Which churches to invite was a more difficult matter. Since the churches to be invited had to be firmly committed to the Reformed confessions, a choice would have to be made out of the whole body of historically Reformed churches. The choice, it was said, would not be simple and easy. The manner of delegating could be left to the participating churches but should take into consideration numerical strength. The agenda of the eventual synod should include matters of common concern and interest — for example, the Reformed position on war and the most recent social, economic, and political issues, movements, and organizations. And most importantly, if the ideal of a Reformed ecumenical synod were to be realized, the synod would have to address what could be done to make the churches' common Reformed confession more influential in our time. Questions regarding the revision and/or extension of the Reformed confession, as well as how to maintain the Reformed doctrinal position over against the modern teaching of evolution, should certainly be put on the agenda of an eventual Reformed ecumenical synod. The synod proposed that its fraternal delegates to the synod of the GKN meeting in 1939, along with representatives from the other two churches, form a preparatory committee to work out the specific details for an eventual council or synod.

At the general synod of the GKN held in August 1939, Henry Beets and Rev. I. Van Dellen met with professors V. Hepp, H. H. Kuyper, S. Greydanus, G. Ch. Aalders, and Dr. G. Keizer, first clerk of the general synod, from the Netherlands; with the Revs. J. G. Fernhout and C. Mak from the East Indies; and with Dr. W. J. Snyman and Dr. S. du Toit from South Africa. This preparatory committee agreed that the international gathering of Reformed churches should assemble in Amsterdam. Although the CRC preferred to call the assembly a council, the name "synod" was finally approved. Its authority, however, would be advisory and not binding on the respective churches, despite what the name "synod" in the Reformed tradition might imply. With little difficulty it was agreed to invite all churches in correspondence with the three organizing churches to become members. Much discussion was devoted to what other churches should be invited. This question was not resolved and other important details were left undecided because of the worsening international situation. The general synod had to temporarily adjourn; the fraternal delegates from abroad returned home.

World War II made the preparations for a Reformed ecumenical synod difficult and the convening of such a synod impossible. Since the GKN could not make the necessary arrangements nor convene a synod, and very likely would not be able to do so until some time after the war, the synod of the CRC authorized its committee for a Reformed ecumenical synod, in consultation with the RCSA, to do the preliminary planning. In 1946 the synod of the CRC approved the committee's work, calling for an ecumenical synod to be convened in Grand Rapids, Michigan. Participation in this so-called "Preparatory Ecumenical Synod" was to be limited to delegations from the GKN, the RCSA, and the CRC. The CRC was to provide the agenda; the synod itself would take up the matter of inviting other churches in the future. In August 1946 the first Reformed Ecumenical Synod (RES), a new undertaking in Reformed catholicity, met as proposed.

Catholicity and Separation: 1944–1966

The Report of 1944

The committee mandated in 1940 to make a thorough study of the CRC's program of church correspondence made its report in 1944.[1] What the committee served up for the synodical delegates — especially the elders, many of whom were uneducated and foreign born — was a tough morsel to chew. Basic terms and concepts such as "sister church" and "correspondence" were given multiple meanings. Almost every statement in the report was carefully nuanced; adjectives and adverbs were used profusely. The fact that the committee submitted a united report, in spite of admittedly different opinions among its members, may have contributed to the report's apparent ambiguities, perhaps even inconsistencies. Emphasizing the unity of the church and the necessity of that unity coming to expression in an undivided church structure, the report reflects the ecumenical spirit of the age. The report also provides an excellent commentary on the CRC's perception of itself and its task in the midst of a multitude of Christian churches.

---

1. The members of the committee were Louis Berkhof, Diedrich H. Kromminga, Jacob T. Hoogstra, Idzerd Van Dellen, and Samuel Volbeda.

Because of the breadth of its assignment, the committee had not yet been able to study the creedal position, doctrinal attitude, and practice of discipline of the many churches that might be considered for official correspondence. In the committee's judgment the first matter to be settled, basic to all the rest, was the question of the basis, aim, scope, and norms for the practice of correspondence with other churches. The report of 1944 addressed itself to these fundamental questions.

While commending the Synod of 1898 for speaking eloquently on the catholicity of the church, the committee judged that its concept of church correspondence was mistaken and seriously flawed. Forty-one years of neglect and ineffectiveness in official correspondence proved the point. The synod in 1898 had mistakenly limited the scope of correspondence, the committee said, to what were called "sister churches" — that is, to Reformed churches, as if other churches were not included in the sisterhood. In so doing the synod had completely lost sight of all non-Reformed churches and, consequently, implicitly denied that they were sister churches. All churches of Christ, the committee contended, were related to one another and therefore sisters. The synod also had not seen things too clearly when it sponsored correspondence with sister churches in America (domestic churches) as well as those in foreign lands. Again the term "sister churches" mistakenly led the church to assume that Reformed churches in America should continue their separate denominational existence rather than to confederate or consolidate in one church structure.

According to the report of 1944 the meaning and understanding of church correspondence as stated in Article 48 of the Church Order of Dort had undergone subtle changes since the Reformation. The fragmentation of the church incidental to the Reformation, the dissolution of the state church, and the erosion of church unity in denominationalism all contributed to altering the original under-

31

standing of the article. These now-settled, abnormal conditions the church had taken as normal. Church correspondence, the committee contended, should be restored to its original meaning and purpose. Historically the Dutch Reformed churches introduced correspondence between particular synods because the government refused to allow the churches to meet in a general synod. Although a poor substitute, correspondence was under the circumstances the next best recourse for the churches. At the time the corresponding churches regarded one another as equals, homogeneous in every respect and virtually constituting one church. By means of correspondence they attempted to stay, act, and cooperate as closely together as possible. This original conception and practice, the report contended, should provide the CRC with the correct understanding and proper pattern for conducting church correspondence. Correspondence should be carried on with churches separated from the CRC only because of geographic distances or differences in language. The CRC and the churches in correspondence with it should sustain a relation of parity and virtual unity. They should also act as one church, short of formal organizational connections prohibited by geographic circumstances and linguistic differences. For all practical purposes the CRC's correspondence should be with foreign churches as truly Reformed as is the CRC.

In addressing the basis, aim, scope, and norms for the practice of church correspondence, the committee did not undertake an exegetical study of Scripture, formulate scriptural principles on the basis of that study, and then apply them to interchurch relations. It rather proceeded on the basis of two fundamental ideas, the one derived from Scripture — thus genuinely representing a scriptural principle — the other merely an assumption representing the committee's opinion. The first was that a plurality of churches in an institutional sense is scripturally improper; Scripture was occasionally cited in support of this idea. The second basic idea was the assumption that the CRC was of all the churches of Christ the closest historical approximation of the ecclesiastical ideal presented in Scripture. Without evidence or proof, the committee stated this assumption frequently, forcefully, and humbly. The committee asserted — without qualification or discrimination — that the conclusions to which it came represented scriptural principles governing the relationship of the CRC to other Christian churches, even though some of the conclusions involved only matters of priority, strategy, and the classification of churches.

According to the report Christian churches were now institutionally separated because of differences in doctrine, worship, and polity. The Word of God, however, does not warrant the radical doctrinal, canonical, and liturgical varieties of ecclesiastical life present in the world today. While Scripture allows some latitude regarding liturgy and polity, it does not permit such extensive differences as, for example, those which set off the hierarchical from the Presbyterian churches or those which distinguish the Roman Catholic mass from public worship in the Reformed tradition. In matters of doctrine Scripture is even more explicit. Because the teaching of Scripture is clear on the fundamentals of church doctrine, polity, and worship, the report, for reasons of principle, vigorously opposed the denominational diversity of the churches. No church honestly professing God's Word as the norm for church life could consistently be indifferent to and disregard this diversity of churches, which in the current sense of the term, the committee contended, was contraband. Every effort should, according to the demands of Scripture, be made to nullify it. No construction of legitimacy should be put upon an illegitimate diversity, even by the use of the term "sister churches." These sisters should really cease to exist because they have no right to be — that is, to deviate — from God's truth and will in doctrine, polity, and worship. In the judgment of the committee, the term "sister church" was properly applicable only to local congregations affiliated in one denomination which could not consolidate and form one congregation. The term should not, however, be applied to similar and parallel denominations unless geographical distances and differences in language rendered denominational separation unavoidable.

In its critique of diversity, the committee was careful to distinguish what it called the absolutist or extremist approach from the moderate or considerate approach. The extremists say that other churches simply are not churches, because in their corporate life they lack scriptural warrant. This reasoning, the committee argued, left no room for imperfect churches. Consequently, the extremists failed to recognize that another church body, whether well organized or not, was still in essence the body of Christ, a company of believers, and therefore deserved to be considered a church. Also, by failing to distinguish more perfect churches from less perfect ones they really maintained that their church was perfect, institutionally speaking, and that other churches lacked every qualification for being called the church.

The moderate or considerate approach, however, was entirely different. This approach proceeded from the assumption that a given church was closer in doctrine, polity, and worship to the scriptural norm for the organized church of Christ than other churches, except, of course, in the case of churches like itself that were separated from it only by geography and language. Churches further from the scriptural pattern are not for that reason no longer to be considered churches. All that can fairly be said of them is that they are less scriptural, though they should be as scriptural. When this position is assumed, the committee said, churches less scripturally sound are not simply disowned or ignored, but at the same time their deficiencies are not condoned or judged unimportant. According to the committee the CRC endorsed the moderate or considerate approach. That it took this position was clear from the fact that the CRC recognized the baptism of all the historical churches of Christendom but declined to enter into organic union with any of them.

The committee attempted to formulate a comprehensive position and program of interchurch relations for the CRC, taking into consideration the biblical teaching regarding the unity and catholicity of the church, scriptural norms for church life, and the committee's assessment of where the CRC stood in relation to these biblical standards. Two matters loomed large in the committee's statement of position and program. The first was that the CRC had an inescapable obligation and responsibility to all Christian churches by the mere fact that they were churches of Christ and therefore could not be disowned or ignored. The second was that the CRC, since it was the closest approximation of the scriptural norm, could not assume an attitude of indifference to its own Reformed faith, polity, and worship. If the CRC simply considered non-Reformed churches as parallel or equal to itself, it would assume an attitude of indifference to its Reformed tradition. The CRC, the committee humbly asserted, was a truly Reformed church, and precisely this fact precluded the possibility that it could deal with non-Reformed churches as though they were Reformed and seek union with them at the cost of fidelity to God and his truth.

The committee very specifically described the CRC's task and aims in interchurch relations when it said: "If we believe that all Christians should be Reformed — and this we profess to believe — then we should try, ecclesiastically as well as otherwise, to win them for the Reformed faith, and so pave the way for eventual union with them, please God."[2] The CRC should therefore exert every effort to achieve church union with other churches of Christ without departing from or surrendering its Reformed identity and integrity in any part of its ecclesiastical life. All truly Reformed churches on the North American continent, the committee was convinced, as a matter of scriptural, divine requirement, must be confederated or structurally united.

2. *Acts of Synod, 1944*, pp. 349-50.

Reformed churches presently divided should not live in separation a day longer than was absolutely necessary. The church's approach to the nominally Reformed and non-Reformed churches, however, had to be different. These churches, by reproof and correction, had to be purged of their unscriptural elements and thus won to the Reformed faith and to eventual union. Organic union was the purpose and goal of interchurch relations. With nominally Reformed and non-Reformed churches reproof and correction were necessary initial steps in the process leading to eventual union.

In laying out its position and program the committee classified the various Christian churches on the basis of their closeness to the CRC. Beginning with the CRC at the center of the ecclesiastical circle, the committee in its classification moved outward to the circumference. The first category were those churches that were historically and officially Reformed but which in the actualities of their life are in fact no longer Reformed. The non-Reformed Protestant churches formed the second group. The Roman Catholic and Oriental churches belonged to a third category.

In the light of this classification of churches, the committee proposed that the CRC's system of official church correspondence be revamped. Using the term "correspondence" in a much broader sense than had previously been done, the committee identified three general types of correspondence:

> A. Correspondence proper, according to Article 48 of the church order, with churches identical with the CRC but with which it cannot unite because of geographical distance and differences in language;
>
> B. Correspondence with Reformed churches that are delinquent either officially in doctrine or in actual practice. This correspondence should be intended to restore them to their original Reformed character and to eventual union on that basis;
>
> C. Correspondence with non-Reformed Protestant

churches. The purpose of this correspondence is to win them to the Reformed faith and to eventual union on that condition.

The committee did not designate a specific type of correspondence with the Roman Catholic and Oriental churches. It did, however, emphatically state that the CRC had a task and responsibility to them. These churches were, after all, churches of Christ and something should be done with them by way of correspondence broadly understood.[3]

In the committee's judgment, the fact that the CRC had an obligation to all Christian churches did not mean that it had to deal with all of them at once. Priorities had to be set. For the present the committee recommended that only type "A" correspondence be undertaken because this was the only kind with which the CRC had experience and for which it was prepared. Type "B" correspondence with delinquent Reformed churches was utterly foreign to the church. The church did not even know with what churches to engage in it or how to go about it. The same was true for type "C" correspondence. The committee summarized its thinking and position in twelve propositions setting forth the biblical basis, aims, and scope of interchurch correspondence.[4]

The report of 1944 said virtually nothing about methodology in interchurch relations, except for a passing reference to the "mistaken methodology of modern ecumenicalism." The committee did recognize that implementing its vision would not be easy. Just how to approach other churches would require special attention and further study. For the present the committee was content merely "to get the right slant on this so-called business of correspondence." The task itself had to be clearly and correctly discerned before the appropriate methodology could be devised. Formulating and stating the general principles governing

3. *Acts of Synod, 1944*, pp. 350-51.
4. *Acts of Synod, 1944*, pp. 357-61.

correspondence was the first and most important item of business. If these principles appealed to the mind and heart of the church it would have a "campaign plan," a foundation upon which progressively to erect a program of correspondence with other churches in a consistently Reformed style. Since the principles were paramount and had to be given time to sink into the consciousness of the church, the committee discouraged hasty action and proposed that the report be referred to the churches for study and comment. A year later the matter would be truly ripe for action. For the present the committee advised the synod neither to resume nor to initiate correspondence with other churches until the CRC arrived at a better understanding of the principles underlying correspondence and the objectives to be pursued in approaching churches on a revised basis.

The report of 1944 dealt with the subject of the catholicity and unity of the church exclusively from the vantage point of interchurch relations intended to produce an organic union between the CRC and other denominations. No consideration was given to membership in ecumenical organizations as possible avenues through which the CRC could even partially and provisionally fulfill its ecumenical calling. The narrowness of the committee's perspective is the more remarkable in light of the fact that the committee already in 1942 had been asked to advise the synod on membership in the American Council of Christian Churches (ACCC), and the fact that the CRC became a member of the National Association of Evangelicals (NAE) in 1943. At the very time the committee submitted its report it was anticipating the formation of a Reformed ecumenical synod consisting of type "A" corresponding churches.

The synod in 1944 did not concur in the committee's advice to postpone action on the report. It rather expressed its appreciation for the thorough report and its agreement with the substance of the twelve propositions, uncritically judging that they presented the biblical principles for church correspondence, even though some of them simply involved matters of priority, strategy, and the classification of churches. The synod did, however, agree not to resume or initiate correspondence with other churches until after the committee completed its study of the churches to be included in official correspondence and how to approach them.

The following year the committee was not prepared to submit anything to synod for action, but it expressed in its report that year the opinion that if a Reformed ecumenical synod came into existence, type "A" correspondence with foreign Reformed churches would disappear. The committee also informed the synod that applying the principles for correspondence involved weighty considerations. The methods to be followed in interchurch relations and the standards to be used when judging whether or not a church was actually Reformed in practice as well as in doctrine were difficult to determine. In 1946 the committee reported that it had made a serious effort but was not yet ready to submit definite recommendations. The principles governing interchurch relations were evidently easier to formulate than to apply and implement. Without the advice and recommendation of the Committee on Ecumenicity and Interchurch Correspondence, the synod decided to send a fraternal delegate to the general assembly of the Orthodox Presbyterian Church (OPC).

In its 1947 report to synod, the committee expressed its extreme unhappiness with this decision, which was in its opinion premature and prejudicial to the study it was making. The committee was, however, ready to report the results of its further study. In striking contrast to the report of 1944, the committee's report on the procedure to be followed in interchurch correspondence was brief, moderate, nonjudgmental, and noticeably tempered by the difficulties involved in moving from the basis and aims to the actual practice of church correspondence. From a purely formal point of view, the committee said, Reformed churches were easy to identify. The problem became complicated and delicate, however, the moment the question was asked whether or not a historically and officially Reformed church was actually Reformed in practice. The committee concluded that answers to this question, which were at the very heart of the purpose of church correspondence, could not be found in official church actions. They would have to be found in other sources through which the committee simply could not search. The committee therefore asked the synod to address a letter embodying the principles set forth in the report of 1944 to a select group of churches, inviting them to begin or to resume correspondence with the CRC. Accepting the invitation, the committee said, would imply official correspondence based on definite principles. The procedure proposed and approved by synod shifted from the CRC to the invited churches the burden of responsibility for determining a church's "Reformedness" and whether in good conscience and on the basis of Scripture it could enter a relationship of fellowship with the CRC. This was a practice regularly followed by other churches and ecumenical organizations.

The Letter of Invitation to Correspondence was modest and cordial. No reference was made to the report of 1944 or its twelve propositions. The letter simply said:

> Permit us to say that in our opinion ecclesiastical fellowship as being grounded in Christian love, should be exercised particularly in the direction of helping each other in remaining true, alike in profession and practice, to the glorious Reformed faith which we hold in common; and in giving heed to each other "that we may live soberly and righteously and godly in this present world, denying ungodliness and worldly lusts" by the grace of God.

The specific terms of the proposed correspondence were:

> 1. Appointment of delegates to each other's supreme judicatories as a token of mutual friendship and interest in the Lord;
> 2. Keeping each other informed of church actions through the exchange of acts of our general synods or assemblies;

3. Bringing to each other's attention our spiritual and ecclesiastical problems together with our attempts at their scriptural solution, and offering each other help upon request;

4. Warning each other in respect to spiritual dangers that arise and spread and imperil the church of Christ;

5. Correcting each other in love in the event of unfaithfulness, whether by commission or remission on the score of profession and/or practice of the faith once delivered to the saints;

6. Consulting each other regarding the eventual revision of our respective ecclesiastical standards.[5]

The extent to which the letter and the terms of correspondence embodied the principles of the report of 1944 is left to the judgment of the reader. The purpose of correspondence — namely, church union — so explicitly stated and forcefully argued in the report of 1944, was noticeably absent from the letter and the specific terms of correspondence.

The letters were sent to the following American denominations: the Reformed Church in America, the Synod of the Reformed Presbyterian Church in North America, the General Synod of the Reformed Presbyterian Church, the Associate Presbyterian Church, the Free Magyar Reformed Church in America (Hungarian Reformed), and the United Presbyterian Church. Letters of invitation were also sent to the following foreign churches: the Christian Reformed Church in the Netherlands (a church consisting of congregations of the Secession of 1834 that did not enter the Union of 1892), the Dutch Reformed Church in South Africa,[6] the Christian Reformed Church of Japan,[7] and the

---

5. *Acts of Synod, 1947*, pp. 215-16.

6. The large Dutch Reformed Church in South Africa did not respond to the invitation and has never become a church in official correspondence or ecclesiastical fellowship with the CRC. Earlier, however, the CRC did have a relationship of correspondence with some of the provincial synods of the DRC.

7. The name should have been the Reformed Church in Japan.

Free Presbyterian Church of Australia. Letters were not sent to the GKN or the RCSA because correspondence with these churches had not entirely lapsed.

Already in 1947 the committee evidently departed from its own 1944 principles governing correspondence by inviting domestic as well as foreign Reformed churches to a relationship of correspondence. In 1947 the committee also reverted to the use of the traditional distinction between sister churches and churches in correspondence. Sister-church relations were described as closer and more intimate and included free pulpit exchange and direct transfer of membership. Upon the recommendation of the committee, the synod invited the OPC to correspondence but denied it the more intimate relationship because the CRC was not sure that the OPC was faithful in church discipline.

In 1948 the Committee on Ecumenicity and Interchurch Correspondence had nothing to report because, it said, it had not received a mandate from the synod. The synod discharged the committee and appointed a new committee of three members — Clarence Bouma, Jacob Hoogstra, and William Rutgers, assisted by the stated clerk, Ralph Danhof (ex-officio) — to carry on the CRC's ecumenical and interchurch relations. For many years these four served as the agency of the CRC to implement the "campaign plan" adopted in 1944. The assignment was indeed large for such a small force.

In 1950 the RCA accepted the invitation to become a church in correspondence, but did not approve all the specific terms of correspondence. In its judgment they were too sweeping in scope and needed to be further defined. In spite of its disappointment, the synod of the CRC decided to exchange fraternal delegates with the RCA.

The Committee on Ecumenicity and Church Corre-

The discrepancy was due either to ignorance or to the fact that the Reformed Church in Japan was in the process of being formed. Later records indicate that the intended church was the Reformed Church in Japan.

spondence continued to work with the twofold classification of "sister churches" and "churches in correspondence." With the exception of the RCA, churches whose historical origins were in the Dutch Reformed tradition and whose confessional standards were the same as those of the CRC were classified as sister churches. Dutch Reformed immigrant churches in Australia, New Zealand, Indonesia, and Ceylon, as well as younger churches in various parts of the world established through the missionary outreach of Dutch Reformed churches, were also placed in this category. Presbyterian churches in America and other parts of the world, most of which had recent secessionist histories and strictly adhered to the Westminster standards, were classified as churches in correspondence.

Membership in the
National Association of Evangelicals

In 1942 and again in 1943 the synod of the CRC received requests and invitations to become a member of the NAE and the American Council of Christian Churches (ACCC). Both organizations came into existence to provide orthodox Protestantism a clear alternative to the Federal Council of Christian Churches (FCCC) and an opportunity to form a united front against the Liberalism rampaging through the ranks of mainline American Protestant denominations. They were also formed to provide evangelical Protestants an agency in which they could band together and with a united voice and through cooperative action accomplish goals that were beyond the reach of individual churches and denominations. Because of the CRC's evangelical character and antipathy for modern Liberalism, the bases and purposes of these organizations appealed to the CRC.

The NAE was better known in the CRC than was the ACCC. Dr. Clarence Bouma played a role in the organization of the NAE, and he and three observer delegates attended the NAE Constitutional Convention in April 1943. The delegates anticipated that the association would probably engage in the work of the church, particularly in doing evangelism, and they acknowledged that the membership of the NAE was more Arminian than Calvinist. Yet their recommendation was to join. The synodical advisory committee, in comparing the NAE and the ACCC, found the two organizations to be essentially the same in doctrine and purpose and judged that rather than two such organizations there should be only one. Since the quality of the leadership and organizational structure of the NAE were better, the committee thought it was the stronger body. The synod, without further investigation and without stating supporting reasons, decided to join the NAE. The record does not indicate whether or not the catholicity of the church or the Reformed understanding of the church were part of the discussions or even influenced the decision.

Every year thereafter and with growing firmness, opponents of the decision asked synod to sever the relationship. The opposition focused on the NAE's program of gospel preaching and the impropriety of churches with radically different theological positions joining together in cooperative activities. Delegates to the national conventions, however, consistently submitted favorable reports. In 1947 and the following year delegates to the national conventions presented both majority reports favoring continued membership and minority reports calling for termination of membership. The 1947 minority report focused especially on two concerns. First, the CRC was the only Calvinist member of the association. Psychologically, the minority contended, the Arminianism of nearly all the other members would have a detrimental effect on members of the CRC. Second, the NAE engaged in gospel-promoting work. Consequently, as long as the CRC was a member of the organization it was a party to and corporately responsible for this work, inspired and promoted by Arminianism.

The majority in 1948 readily acknowledged that the NAE, like much of the American church world, was largely Arminian. Delegates to the national conventions from the CRC were, however, sufficiently grounded in the Reformed faith, the majority said, so as not to "be swept off their feet by attending a convention." The majority also attempted to answer the questions raised regarding loyalty to the Reformed faith and the propriety of membership in a doctrinally diverse and mixed organization. Previously, the majority said, the CRC had avoided these problems by isolating itself. Admittedly, the Reformed fathers would not within their own denominational life have considered cooperating with Arminians. Nor would the majority. But working together for the protection of common interests and the promotion of the kingdom of God in a general sense was another matter. The whole purpose of the NAE was to promote the cause of Christ. In this cause the CRC was, as part of the holy catholic church, one with the other members. In the face of these conflicting reports, the synod appointed a special committee to study the NAE and review the CRC's membership in it.

In 1949 the study committee presented majority and minority reports.[8] The majority recommended terminating membership, but was careful to point out that their recommendation was not based on the suspicion that Fundamentalists were not Christians, or on any aversion to interdenominational cooperation, or on the belief that the CRC should isolate itself. The recommendation was based on two considerations: first, that Fundamentalism was theologically, philosophically, ethically, and ecclesiastically neither Calvinistic nor in the mainstream of evangelical Protestantism. The second was that the NAE was fundamentalistic — as its

8. Members of the majority committee were Harold Dekker, Peter H. Eldersveld, W. Harry Jellema, and Peter Van Tuinen. The minority were Clarence Bouma and John Gritter.

sectarian constituency, its attenuated statement of faith, and its confused witness testified. The majority asked the synod to terminate membership lest the church's Reformed witness be confused, submerged, and impaired, and lest the growth of Fundamentalism accelerate in the CRC.

The majority report was counterbalanced by a minority report and the report of the delegates to the last national convention who, once again, unanimously supported continued membership. The minority recommended that the CRC not only remain a member but attempt to make the NAE more effective and productive. They argued that membership in the association was consistent with the church's confession of one holy catholic church, that it satisfied a deep-felt desire for cooperation with others of "like common faith," and that it provided the CRC an opportunity to make its understanding of Christianity known in the American world. Withdrawal, the minority contended, would only comfort isolationists and modernists and detract from the denomination's confession regarding the church.

The synodical committee to which the two reports were presented for advice noted the radical differences between them. There was no agreement on such basic concepts as Fundamentalism, catholicity, isolation, witness, and the Protestant tradition. In the judgment of the advisory committee neither report adequately set forth or defined the basic scriptural and creedal principles in terms of which affiliation should be judged. Rather than acting on the conflicting recommendations of the reports, the advisory committee recommended that synod appoint another special study committee to search out and set forth the basic scriptural and creedal statements relevant to the whole question of interchurch relations and to formulate principles to guide the church in matters pertaining to interchurch affiliation. The advisory committee further suggested that the inquiry include such important matters as the following:

1. What is to be understood by the scriptural teaching concerning the "Oneness of the Body of Christ," and what are its implications for the historical and institutional manifestation of the church? Or, what is the nature and measure and what are the conditions of our ecumenical responsibility?

2. In how far, and in what manner, may a church which is committed to definite creeds, and which regards itself obliged to exercise its witness in terms of these creeds, unite in common witness with those who differ from these creeds?

3. What is to be understood by the scriptural teaching concerning the "Unity of Faith" and what are its implications for interchurch fellowship and witness?[9]

The advisory committee thought that the church did not have clearly defined principles to guide its practice in interchurch fellowship and witness. The recommended study and definition, the committee judged, was appropriate and necessary in a day when all Christendom was concerned theoretically and practically with the issues involved in ecumenicity. The synod adopted the recommendation of the advisory committee.

The committee studying the NAE did not refer to the report of 1944 in either of its reports, nor did the advisory committee; evidently it had been forgotten. These committees must have either been unimpressed with the scriptural basis of the report of 1944 or considered it irrelevant for evaluating membership in ecumenical organizations.

The mandate the synod gave the study committee in 1949 was broad and good and the requested study was much needed.[10] If the committee had built on the foundations of the catholic vision so clearly and forthrightly stated in the report of 1944, and if it had articulated a biblically and confessionally based ecumenical calling and responsi-

9. *Acts of Synod, 1949*, pp. 23-24.
10. The members of the committee were Martin Monsma, Peter Holwerda, George Gritter, John Kromminga, John Luchies, and William Hendriksen.

bility for the church, applicable to the ecumenical organizations arising in the middle of the twentieth century, the committee could have provided the CRC with a chart and compass to set the course and guide it through the burgeoning ecumenical age. This the committee did not do. It made no attempt to define the basic concepts and terms about which there were such radical differences of opinion in the reports of the previous study committee. Narrowly interpreting its mandate, the committee simply attempted to search out and set forth scriptural and creedal principles without indicating their relevance for interchurch relations or ecumenical organizations. The committee's work was superficial; some of its opinions, especially those regarding catholicity and separation, were wrong. Many of the questions that the synod asked the study committee to investigate it scrupulously avoided out of fear of prejudicing the decision on membership in the NAE.

In the first section of the report, "Scriptural Principles," the committee said the "rise of denominations belonged to the post-biblical era." From this incontrovertible fact, it then concluded that the teachings of Scripture had no direct bearing on interdenominational relationships. The statement, standing without further comment, suggests that the fundamental criticism of ecclesiastical diversity on the basis of the Bible so emphatically stated in the report of 1944 had not yet sunk very deeply into the consciousness of the CRC. Read in the light of the pervasive denominational diversity of the church in modern times, the statement in effect biblically sanctioned the status quo, undermined catholicity, and desensitized the CRC to the need to express visibly the unity of Christ's church through church union or ecumenical organizations.

In the second section of the report dealing with the creeds and Reformed confessions, the committee said that Lord's Day 21 of the Heidelberg Catechism and Article 27 of the Belgic Confession expressed the church's faith concerning the one holy catholic church as the ideal church —

that is, the body of the redeemed of all ages visible only to God. Article 28 then moved the thought forward to the church as it appears on earth. The nature of this church was then set forth in Article 29, which dealt with the marks of the true church. The committee concluded that these confessional teachings did not present "what may be considered the primary or secondary teachings of the Scripture. Consequently they threw no particular light on interchurch relations."[11] The Canons of Dort, the committee said, made it very clear that there could be no church union with those who hold Arminian teachings.

The committee was seriously in error in its understanding of the Reformed doctrine of the church as presented in the confessional standards. Neither the Reformed confessions nor the ancient creeds have an article affirming an invisible church. Lord's Day 21 of the Catechism and Article 27 of the Belgic Confession express faith in one holy catholic church as a historically existing community of true Christian believers dispersed throughout the world. The Reformed confessions neither anticipate nor affirm ecclesiastical pluriformity or denominationalism. Article 28 refers to

11. *Acts of Synod, 1950,* p. 385. In its interpretation of the Catechism and these articles of the Belgic Confession, the committee was probably influenced by Abraham Kuyper's conception of the church. Kuyper made extensive use of the distinction between the invisible and the visible church. Although essentially pre-temporal and supra-historical, the invisible church through its members formed the essence of the temporal and historical church. As a matter of principle Kuyper opted for ecclesiastical pluriformity or denominationalism. In his judgment all the attributes of the church belonged to the invisible church with the exception of apostolicity, a Roman Catholic innovation. Kuyper did not base his preference for denominationalism on Scripture or the Reformed confessions. He derived it from a philosophical principle rooted in nineteenth-century naturalism. He argued that the church in New Testament times began as a complete unity, as do all forms of life. But what began with uniformity, by higher development through conflict and division had to pass over, in keeping with God's ordinances for life, into multiformity and diversity. All organisms, the church included, were subject to this law of development and differentiation.

the very same church as that confessed and described in the previous article. It asserts that outside the one holy catholic church there is no salvation and that believers are obliged to join it, keep its unity, and separate from those who do not belong to the church. Contrary to the committee's opinion Article 29 does not set forth the nature of the church but deals with the marks, indicia, signs, or indicators of the presence of the true church. Where the marks are present, believers may be confident the catholic church is present. The synod in 1950 did not act on the study committee's report but referred it to the churches for study.

The report evidently was not given much study by the churches. In 1951 the synodical advisory committee asked the synod to postpone action on the principles bearing on interchurch affiliation and, consequently, on membership in the NAE. The biblical and creedal principles were extremely important and had not yet received ample study. The synod, however, was more concerned to deal with the burr under its saddle than with the scriptural and creedal principles. The advisory committee's recommendation was tabled; the principles were never discussed or debated.

Progressive elements in the CRC critical of the Fundamentalism of the NAE, and the church's radio minister, Rev. Peter Eldersveld, who adamantly opposed continued membership, combined forces with strict confessional isolationists in a successful effort at the Synod of 1951 to terminate affiliation. No grounds were given for the decision to sever the relationship. The synod did, however, send a letter to the officers of the NAE informing them of its decision. The letter was not printed in the *Acts of Synod*.

Subsequent synods received communications objecting to the decision, because the Synod of 1951 had not first acted on the report on the principles for interchurch affiliation and because no grounds were given for the decision. To silence the critics, the synod in 1954 printed the letter:

After a lengthy discussion and serious consideration, it became apparent that our membership in the association is not a happy one. The Christian Reformed Church is a close-knit denomination with a very specific creed and a practice based upon and in harmony with this creed. Membership in the NAE, loosely organized and without a well-defined program of action, easily does lead and in the past has led to embarrassment and difficulty. It was felt that the testimony the Christian Reformed Church is called to bring in this day and in this world is in danger of being weakened by continued membership in the NAE.[12]

Church Union Conversations with the Reformed Presbyterian and Orthodox Presbyterian Churches

For the purpose of carrying on what were called "ecumenical and closer fellowship conversations," the synod of the CRC in 1956 appointed committees to meet with similar committees of the Reformed Presbyterian Church in North America (Covenanters) and the OPC. The initiative for the talks with the Reformed Presbyterians came from them; two years earlier they had decided to make a beginning toward church union with other churches on a scriptural basis. Conversations with the Reformed Presbyterians lasted five years. Committee reports to CRC synods indicate that in matters of theology and doctrine the two churches were in complete agreement. While recognizing differences in church government — the Reformed Presbyterians being of Scottish Presbyterian origin — the CRC committee judged that these differences were not significant obstacles to eventual union. The insurmountable difficulties and problems were in the areas of practice, particularly public worship and the Reformed Presbyterians' position on political dissent. The Covenanters sang only psalms without the

12. *Acts of Synod, 1954*, p. 175.

use of musical instruments. They also remained in a state of political dissent, officially refusing to allow their members to vote or hold public office until the Lordship of Christ was, by way of amendment, added to the American Constitution.

For the Covenanters these differences were not matters of mere practice or custom but of principle. The committee representing the CRC concluded that were it not for these traditional positions and practices the Reformed Presbyterian Church could unite with the CRC. Since, however, the Covenanters would likely continue to cling tenaciously to their distinctive practices, the committee recommended that the present conversations be discontinued and that relationships between the two churches be again placed on the agendas of the denominational committees for interchurch relations. New efforts toward closer affiliation would have to await the initiative of the Reformed Presbyterian Church. The synod in 1961 followed the committee's advice.

The initiative for conversations with the OPC came from the CRC. Requests for closer relations from within the CRC and the fact that a sister church, the GKN, had recognized the OPC as a sister church provided the occasion for these conversations.

In recommending joint discussions, the Committee on Ecumenicity and Church Correspondence was motivated by the teaching of Scripture and the report of 1944. Both implied axiomatically that believers who were spiritually one should, if at all possible, be organically one. Organic union was the ideal. The committee reportedly struggled with how to proceed. After considering a variety of options, it decided the best procedure would be to have committees appointed by the major assemblies of each church sit at the same table on an equal basis. This mode of action was considered efficient, noncontroversial, mutually instructive, fraternal, and confidential. It was also commonly used in ecumenical circles. Even though its results in the World

Council of Churches (WCC) might not be applauded, the committee nevertheless thought the method could be an effective means to obtain more limited ecumenical goals.

Committees appointed by the synod of the CRC and the general assembly of the OPC formed a joint committee to consider closer relations between the churches. The Committee on Ecumenicity and Interchurch Correspondence continued to monitor the work of the representatives of the CRC. Upon the recommendation of the joint committee, the synod and general assembly adopted two resolutions, one clearly affirming catholicity, the other indicating the importance of realistically facing and resolving differences in achieving church union. The resolutions were the following:

> 1. In view of the unity of the body of Christ and in view of the basic community that exists between the Christian Reformed Church and the Orthodox Presbyterian Church in doctrine, polity, and practice, an obligation rests upon these two churches to make every legitimate endeavor to bring the unity and community to their consistent expression in organic union between the two denominations.
> 2. It would, however, be prejudicial to this ultimate objective and unrealistic to fail to take account of differences that exist between the two denominations, and it is necessary to face these differences and explore ways and means of resolving them.[13]

As a result of progress in the consultations, the joint committee was specifically mandated in 1959 to work for union.

Differences between the Presbyterian and Reformed systems of church government soon surfaced and were considered the greatest obstacles to a union of the two denominations. In 1962 the representatives of the CRC requested permission to explore in general the distinction made, but not elaborated, in the report of 1944 between essentials and

13. *Acts of Synod, 1957*, p. 103.

nonessentials in doctrine, polity, and liturgy. The synod did not grant the committee's request, but asked the committee for the time being to give priority only to the question of essentials and nonessentials in polity, because of the pivotal role differences in church government played in the conversations.

The joint committee made good progress. In 1966 the synod of the CRC noted with appreciation that the representatives of the OPC were requesting their general assembly to declare that the joint committee should work toward the definite goal of organic union. The synod also encouraged cooperative activities between the two denominations, such as pulpit exchanges, youth programs, conferences, and cooperation in home missions and publishing. Sensing that organic union was within grasp, the synod instructed its committee to define the remaining areas of disagreement and to suggest ways to bring about organic union.

The following year, however, the merger effort took a turn for the worse and from that point inexorably deteriorated. In 1967 the general assembly of the OPC retired its representatives from the joint committee and appointed new members, giving them the mandate to investigate trends toward Liberalism in the CRC. In 1970 the OPC laid before the joint committee a document entitled "Unfamiliar Utterances." The OPC's fraternal delegate, Rev. John Mitchell, identified these utterances for the benefit of the synod of the CRC. They touched such matters as (1) the infallibility of Scripture, including both its authority and its inerrancy, (2) the particular atonement of Christ as it relates to all men individually, (3) the special creation of man, involving the Genesis account and evolutionary theory, and (4) the propriety of considering membership in the WCC.

Confronted with a discouraging report from the representatives of the CRC on the joint committee, the synodical advisory committee in 1971 observed that after many years of progress in working toward unity, the joint committee recently had made no progress. Difficulties had arisen on two fronts. Within the CRC eventual union was no longer a burning issue. The committee said the synod must examine its own state of mind and heart about the issue, because undefined and unspecific desires for church unity were not enough. The church had to deal very specifically with the fact that intense interest in uniting with the OPC simply did not exist. From the OPC side, the joint committee continually faced OPC allegations of Liberalism within the CRC. These allegations, the advisory committee said, were not based on official synodical pronouncements but on articles written by church leaders and even on reported conversations with Christian Reformed persons.

The advisory committee also commented on the problem the representatives of the CRC had in serving on the joint committee. They had become "unequally yoked" as a result of the decisions of the general assembly in 1967, which changed not only the personnel of the joint committee but also its mandate. Investigating Liberalism in the CRC had now become in practice the committee's primary agenda. This change forced the representatives of the CRC into a defensive posture, shifted the focus away from eventual union, and imposed an undue emphasis on defending statements and answering allegations dealing with subtle differences of opinion that frequently were merely semantic in nature.

A letter from the OPC expressing a positive attitude toward the consultations and presumably a different outlook led the synod to continue the committee for another year. The following year the synod encouraged the churches to hold to the ultimate hope of organic union of "all like-minded churches on a scriptural basis." The imperative for such union, the synod said, had been effectively stated in the report of 1944. The synod then decided for the time being to postpone union discussions with the OPC. After sixteen years of intense effort and negotiation, the CRC's only serious attempt to implement the scriptural principle of organic union with another American church — Reformed in doctrine, polity, and practice — ended in failure. The synod placed all matters of contact with the OPC with its Interchurch Relations Committee.[14]

Investigating the Possibility of Membership in Ecumenical Organizations

Early in the second half of the twentieth century the critical world situation, the obvious vitality of the ecumenical movement within Christianity, and classic Reformed ecclesiology — in which the catholicity of the church was an important component — combined to compel the CRC to reflect on its ecumenical calling. In 1957 the synod asked its standing Committee on Ecumenicity and Interchurch Correspondence to make a study of existing ecumenical organizations for the purpose of advising the synod whether or not the CRC should become a member of one of them.[15] In its report to the next synod the committee commented on both the church's ecumenical responsibility and the urgency of the present world situation. The ecumenical question, the committee said, was the single most important issue confronting the churches today. The CRC would have to accept and deal with this fact in a responsible way. The urgency of the world situation made complacency unpardonable. Communism and the increasing power and influence of the Roman Catholic Church were specifically mentioned as especially dangerous elements in contemporary life that might demand cooperative Christian action and witness by Protestant Christian churches.

14. The name of the Committee on Ecumenicity and Church Correspondence was changed to the Interchurch Relations Committee in 1966.
15. At the time, the members of the committee were William H. Rutgers, Jacob T. Hoogstra, Ralph J. Danhof, and Martin Monsma.

In pursuing its mandate the committee informed the Synod of 1958 that it had already received materials from the National Association of Evangelicals, the International Council of Christian Churches, the World Presbyterian Alliance (formerly the Alliance of Reformed Churches holding the Presbyterian system), and the World Council of Churches. Materials had also been requested from the American Council of Christian Churches and from the National Council of Christian Churches. The committee promised to review the constitutions, statements of purpose, and practices of all these organizations. The committee also said it would look at the impact these organizations made on the public through their pronouncements and activities. In the light of these thorough inquiries the committee would then try to ascertain whether membership in them would help or hinder the CRC in fulfilling its calling and ministry.

Before digging into the sizable agenda it set for itself, the committee gave some indication of its thinking. False ecumenicity without further definition, it said, was no ecumenicity but a deception. Strengthening and promoting the Reformed Ecumenical Synod (RES) was urgent. The committee also informed the synod that it accepted the principle, clearly presented in the report of 1944, that the CRC begin first with the church or churches closest to it and then widen the circle to more distant churches. Evidently the committee thought the principles of the report of 1944 could be applied to ecumenical organizations as well as to churches.

In 1959 the committee reported the results of its investigation into the World Presbyterian Alliance (WPA), clearly indicating in its report that the committee was not in favor of the CRC becoming a member of an ecumenical body of Reformed churches that was not committed to strict adherence to the Reformed confessional standards. Interestingly, the report did not refer to the report of 1944, nor did it affirm an ecumenical responsibility to churches that were historically and officially Reformed but not so in actual practice. The committee judged the Statement of Basis in the constitution of the WPA too dogmatically indistinct, especially when viewed in the context of contemporary theology. Because the alliance urged its member churches to express their unity with all the churches of Christ by becoming members of the WCC, the committee concluded that it was too closely affiliated with the World Council and promoted an ecumenical rather than a distinctively Reformed vision. The committee also objected to the fact that the WPA was a theologically mixed company consisting of "Liberals, Middle-of-the-Roaders, Barthians, and Orthodox believers in the infallible inspiration of the Bible." The undesirability of membership in this theologically diverse body was intensified by the fact that churches from both sides of the Iron Curtain were members. For these reasons the committee urged the synod not to apply for membership.

The committee was careful to point out, however, that the position it had assumed was compatible with the church's obligation to witness. When expressed in a Christian spirit and with a clear conscience, nonmembership itself could be a more vocal and effective witness than joining a large ecumenical organization.

Probably due to an oversight, the synod did not act on the recommendation of the committee, but the following year the synod decided not to apply for membership in the WPA. The synod did not support its decision with the committee's negative judgments. The only reason given for the decision was that membership in the alliance had far-reaching implications that had not yet been sufficiently explored to warrant final action.

In 1960 the committee reported nothing on its study and review of ecumenical organizations. A year later, it submitted a report on the NAE which did not subject the NAE to the critical inquiry and review that the committee had previously set for all the ecumenical organizations it was committed to investigate. The committee approached the NAE from the vantage point of the CRC's former membership and argued for reaffiliation.

In making the case for reaffiliation, the committee did not mention the report of 1944, but rather argued from the CRC's faith in a holy catholic church and the urgent need in the contemporary world for a united witness on the part of all who were committed to the Word of God. The catholicity of the church required the CRC to recognize and participate in a broader ecumenicity than that represented in the RES. Communism, atheistic philosophy, paganism, Roman Catholicism, modernism, and the social and moral disintegration so characteristic of modern life also compelled the denomination realistically to acknowledge that it could not single-handedly wage war for Christianity. In addition to these basic arguments, the committee contended that the CRC implicitly had accepted the propriety of functional or cooperative ecumenical action from the use it had made in its own ministry of the various commissions and affiliates of the NAE. Finally, the committee said, membership afforded an opportunity for Reformed witness. The CRC with its strong creedal position and Calvinistic leadership could fill an important role in the association and make a positive contribution to it.

But these arguments were not sufficient to alter the churches' stance regarding the NAE; the synod decided not to reaffiliate. One reason was given for the decision: the NAE was not an exclusively ecclesiastical organization.

The Committee on Ecumenicity and Interchurch Correspondence, in carrying out the mandate given it by the Synod of 1957, never reported the results of its study and review of the other ecumenical organizations on which it informed the synod it was gathering information. By 1961 the committee had evidently decided to ignore its previous commitment and to shift the focus of its work.

In the concluding section of its 1961 report the committee again reminded the synod that in pursuing its mandate it was being guided by the report of 1944. For the synod's information the committee cited the earlier report's twelve propositions governing correspondence with other churches. The committee then listed the CRC's foreign sister churches and both the foreign and American churches with which the church had a relationship of official correspondence. The committee also listed a number of churches that it was studying with a view to possibly inviting them to become churches in correspondence. Included in this list were the Presbyterian Church in the U.S. (Southern Presbyterian) and the United Presbyterian Church in the U.S.A. The committee never reported to the synod the results of these studies.

Catholicity and Separation: 1966–1987

World Council of Churches

In 1966 the Committee on Ecumenicity and Interchurch Correspondence underwent a partial face-lift. Some new members were appointed to the committee and it was given a new name, the Interchurch Relations Committee.[1] The new committee immediately confronted a new problem. After many years of studying diversity and ecumenicity, the Reformed Churches in the Netherlands (GKN) adopted a resolution stating that it had no objections on the basis of principle to membership in the WCC. The GKN did not immediately apply for membership in the WCC but decided to wait until its own congregations and the member churches of the RES were given an opportunity to express their judgment on the matter. The Interchurch Relations Committee thought that the careful preparatory study and resolution of the GKN called for a no less thorough study and responsible judgment on the part of the CRC. If the CRC felt constrained to differ with its sister church, it should

1. The members of the committee were Jacob T. Hoogstra, Clarence Boomsma, John Kromminga, Lawrence Veltkamp, and the stated clerk, Ralph Danhof (ex officio).

do so only by presenting a careful argument that refuted the evaluation and resolution of the GKN. If, however, the synod did not disagree with the resolution, its judgment would possibly have implications for the CRC's relationship to the WCC. In this way the stage was set for thorough study and, possibly, clear alternatives. The synod appointed a study committee with a twofold mandate: first, to define the CRC's position regarding the WCC, and second, to prepare a statement as the church's reply to the GKN. Since the GKN was waiting for an answer, and the RES, which was scheduled to meet in Amsterdam in 1968, would again have the question of membership in the World Council on its agenda, the synod requested the special study committee to report to the synod, if at all possible, in 1967.

In this way the issue of membership in the WCC was thrust upon the CRC from outside. Due to its previous history of secession and isolation, the CRC did not participate in the struggle and the experience of the churches that combined forces in the formation of the council. The scandal of a divided Christian church and the intensely felt need for cooperative action and witness after fifty years of international unrest and turbulence (which provided the motivation for organizing the WCC) simply were not part of the CRC's experience. The threats to Christianity represented in the revival of the world religions, in alien ideologies, and in modern secularism — so prominent in the thinking of early leaders in the ecumenical movement — were perceived in the CRC to some degree as dangers to the Reformed faith. They were not, however, perceived as threats to the life and witness of the universal church of Christ calling for cooperative action on the part of all churches, including the CRC.

During the first decades of its existence, the WCC was little known and much feared by certain evangelical churches in America and the CRC, whose ecumenical experience had been limited to the RES.

The WCC was a large and very complex organization. During the 1950s and 1960s, it was — and since then has continued to be — very much in process and flux, especially in matters concerning its own ecclesiastical identity and the specific nature of the unity it embodies and seeks to express. In 1950 a statement on "The Church, the Churches, and the World Council of Churches" (the so-called Toronto Statement) was issued in an effort to remove ambiguities and uncertainties regarding the nature of the council and the unity it expressed. The Statement of Basis was amended in New Delhi in 1961. Both the Toronto Statement and the amendment suggest that the council was struggling with the question of its own ecclesiastical character and the implications of membership in the organization. The CRC's limited ecumenical experience and knowledge of the council, on the one hand, and the council's complexity and ongoing search for a clearer perception of its own identity, on the other, made the committee's assignment large and difficult.

Unfortunately, the study committee had to work under severe time limitations, which not only restricted the thoroughness of the committee's study but also forced the committee rather early in its discussions to decide the specific matters on which the synod asked for a judgment. The one pressing and unavoidable question was whether or not membership in the WCC was permissible for a confessional Reformed church. On this question the committee divided, splitting into majority and minority groups.[2] The reports later submitted to synod indicate that, in spite of some differences in nuance and accent, there was broad consensus on many important matters, such as the ecumenical calling of the church, the CRC's previous isolation, and the relevant biblical teaching on the church. Both reports indicate loyalty and commitment to the Reformed faith and

2. Representing the majority were Peter Y. De Jong, Henry Evenhouse, Fred H. Klooster, Joel Nederhood, Louis Praamsma, and Richard S. Wierenga. Clarence Boomsma and John Kromminga formed the minority.

Christian Reformed tradition and a desire to continue to build on those foundations. What the one report regarded as fundamental objections precluding membership in the WCC the other considered of such a serious nature that it advised against membership. The church's ecumenical responsibility highlighted in the one report was acknowledged to be a very important concern in the other.

If the study committee had been given more time, it could perhaps have integrated into one report the two best and most comprehensive biblical and exegetical studies yet to appear in the CRC on the nature of the church and its ecumenical calling. On the basis of this biblical material and the doctrine of the church reflected in the creeds and confessions, the committee could conceivably have formulated principles to guide the church in ecumenical and interchurch relations, including the goals to be pursued and the appropriate methodologies to be followed. Then, after completing this foundational work, it could have addressed itself specifically to the question of membership in the WCC and, if necessary, submitted separate reports on that issue.

The majority took the position that a truly Reformed church may not seek membership in the World Council; the minority contended that membership, while permissible, was not advisable. Each committee marshalled, organized, and presented data in such a way as to make a compelling case for its position. Both reports were for the most part comprehensive, together numbering 106 pages. They were also penetrating in their analyses and presented well-developed arguments. Differences between the reports stemmed in no small measure from the fact that the WCC was still very much in flux on crucial matters and ambiguous in its own statements. The majority was inclined, from the vantage point of Reformed orthodoxy, to interpret most unfavorably unknown quantities, unclear statements, and uncertain implications regarding the WCC and membership in it, while the minority tried to understand them in the most favorable light. The value of the reports is not so much in their contrasting analysis and evaluation of the World Council as in the manner in which they reflect recent thinking in the CRC concerning the church's ecumenical calling and what is involved in ecumenical relationships.

The majority report took its starting point in selected past synodical decisions. These decisions, for the most part, expressed the CRC's secessionist and separatist mentality in interchurch and ecumenical relations. Some earlier synodical decisions and committee recommendations affirming the catholicity of the church and the need for broader ecumenical relationships were omitted. For example, the 1964 decision of synod adopting the judgment of the RES (Grand Rapids, 1963) was not included. Responding to the GKN's study "Ecumenicity and Pluriformity," the RES had expressed "its appreciation of the vast amount of valuable material in this study, particularly on the nature of the church in relation to ecumenicity; that the church of Jesus Christ is one, that the church in its visible aspect must strive to manifest this oneness, and that in consequence membership in the RES, important though it is, does not exhaust the ecumenical task of a Reformed church."[3] The twelve propositions of the report of 1944 were quoted in full. In contrast, the minority report took its point of departure from the ecumenical calling of the church, addressing itself first to the scriptural teaching on the subject and then to what previous CRC synods had said about the church's ecumenical calling. Finally, the minority presented the official statements of the WCC, virtually without comment.

Both reports unequivocally affirmed the doctrine of the one holy catholic and apostolic church, which was represented as a community of believers presently existing in local congregations and in a worldwide fellowship. Both viewed the unity of the church as given in Christ and firmly established on apostolic teaching and doctrinal truth. The reports concurred in the judgment that the unity given in

3. *Acts of Synod, 1964*, p. 77.

Christ demanded visible expression and had to be preserved and defended by separation from the world, unbelief, and false teaching.

The reports, however, presented some striking differences in their perceptions of biblical teaching, and these differences led to quite different conclusions. The contrast is most apparent in how the two reports address the fellowship of Christ's church. According to the majority, church fellowship in the New Testament is intimate and inseparably connected with apostolic teaching. Conversely, true Christian fellowship, biblically understood, demands withholding fellowship from unbelievers and those unfaithful to the gospel to the point of separation. Paul, the report stated, did not hesitate to pronounce an anathema upon those who pervert sound doctrine, such as the Judaizers in the churches of Galatia. And the glorified Savior rebuked the angels of the churches of Pergamum and Thyatira for tolerating false teachings. The majority concluded its treatment of the biblical material with the statement: "From all this it is apparent that according to Scripture true church fellowship always includes a denunciation of error and ungodliness and a calling to those who would be faithful to Christ and his gospel to separate themselves from all who persist in these sins."[4]

According to the minority the New Testament emphasizes that the unity and fellowship of Christ's church is constantly threatened, and therefore believers have an obligation to strive for unity and, as much as possible, manifest it in the world. In addition to doctrinal error and unbelief, the New Testament identifies sin and failure in love as divisive factors disrupting church unity and fellowship. Unity that is not in Christ, not in truth, and not in love is false unity and a destroyer of true unity. Therefore, to preserve and maintain true unity the church must indeed separate itself from heresy and evil. The minority added,

4. *Acts of Synod, 1967*, pp. 409-10.

however, that such separation, according to the New Testament, was also limited, provisional, and hopefully aimed at the restoration of true fellowship. With patience, tolerance, and forbearance every effort should be made to correct and restore the errant and unfaithful. The minority acknowledged that church fellowship could be broken by heresy and sin in extreme instances when the very life of the church was threatened, but otherwise the church must seek to preserve and promote fellowship with the erring and weak who are still in some sense brethren and not enemies. Paul and Christ set an example for dealing with churches that are defective in their understanding of the truth and failing in their practices. The apostle did not hesitate to call the churches of Galatia brethren, nor did he suggest breaking fellowship with them. Corinth, for all its divisions, doctrinal deviations, and immorality was still addressed as the church of God. Likewise, Christ continued to love and bring his Word to Thyatira and Sardis, in spite of their sin and deadness. In striking contrast to the majority, the minority concluded their treatment of the biblical material with the statement: "We have a responsibility to all the churches of Christ in order that we may all be one in Christ, in truth, and in love, and that our fellowship with Christ and with His body may be perfect."[5]

The minority report took into consideration the doctrinal statements on the church found in the ancient ecumenical creeds and the Reformed confessions. On the basis of Scripture it also rather soundly criticized the present denominational plurality of the church. The New Testament, it said, knows only the church of Jesus Christ and does not allow for many churches differing in faith and lacking in love for each other. To be indifferent to the broken unity of the church of Christ is to continue in sin, to make the prayer of Christ of no effect, and to be disobedient to Christ's command to love. The majority, in contrast,

5. *Acts of Synod, 1967*, p. 453.

nowhere specifically dealt with the creeds and confessions, nor did it express a forthright critical judgment of the plurality of church denominations.

The majority voiced two fundamental criticisms of the WCC as presently organized and constituted. Almost all of their negative judgments regarding the council and membership in it came from these two objections. The first was that the World Council was an inclusive organization consisting of all types and kinds of churches. It embraced within its membership churches whose official doctrinal position was declared heretical by the ancient ecumenical councils, and others with doctrines the orthodox churches have more recently declared to be in conflict with the teaching of Scripture, such as Pelagianism, semi-Pelagianism, Arminianism, Liberalism, neo-orthodoxy, and neo-Liberalism. The council even included some churches to which the name "modernist" was fully or partially applicable.

The second fundamental criticism was that the WCC claimed to be a "Council of Churches," defined itself as a "fellowship of churches," and represented itself, at least provisionally, as a manifestation of the unity given in Christ. The majority took the WCC's claim, definition, and self-representation with utmost seriousness. The majority then weighed, tested, and evaluated the WCC collectively and its member churches individually by the same biblical and confessional Reformed norms and standards for the church in doctrine and in life with which the majority was acquainted and which had always been applied to the church in the strict confessional Reformed tradition. A Reformed church, the majority said, had to judge whether it could in truth acknowledge that all member churches were indeed churches individually, manifestations of the body of Christ possessing the unity given in Christ. The majority sincerely doubted that this could honestly be said. If not all member churches were in fact churches of Christ, the World Council could not rightly claim to be a council of churches.

The majority also insisted that the WCC's claim to be

68

a fellowship of churches and a true manifestation of unity in Christ, albeit provisionally, had to be tested by the same rigorous standards. If a Reformed church could not affirm that one of the member churches was truly a church of Jesus Christ, possessing unity in him, it could not affirm that the World Council as a whole possessed and provisionally manifested the unity given in Christ. Neither could a Reformed church acknowledge that the council was a fellowship of churches if one of the member churches did not possess the unity given in Christ. By including in its fellowship a single member not possessing unity in Christ, the council ceased to be a fellowship of churches. The majority drew the lines even tighter. By becoming a member of the World Council per se, a church implicitly affirmed that all the other members were churches of Christ, shared the unity given in him, and now manifested that unity in the World Council. No Reformed church, the majority asserted, could make such a declaration regarding liberal or modernist churches. The wide spectrum of contradictory theological positions represented in the council itself and the clearly heretical character and equivocal stance of many member churches with respect to the doctrine of Scripture indicated the kind of situation a Reformed church confronted in such an inclusivistic and diverse ecumenical body.

The majority subjected other specific features and aspects of the WCC to scathing criticism. The Statement of Basis,[6] the majority contended, was inadequate, equivocal, ambiguous, and too general in view of the doctrinal errors within the churches today. Furthermore, the World Council did not maintain the basis because it allowed each member church to decide whether or not it could sincerely accept the basis rather than to assume for itself the responsibility for that

6. The basis as amended is, "The World Council of Churches is a fellowship of churches which confess the Lord Jesus Christ as God and Saviour according to the Scriptures and therefore seek to fulfill together their common calling to the glory of the one God, Father, Son, and Holy Spirit."

judgment. Neither did the basis function in a really meaningful way, as was evident from the fact that though most member churches did not exercise church discipline and were quite mixed theologically, the council refused to expel them.

In the opinion of the majority, the social and political activities and declarations of the World Council were obstacles to membership for a Reformed church. The social services and programs of the council reflected at least some of the "social gospel" thinking of the older Liberalism; the principles of state socialism shaped the council's economic and political thinking. While recognizing the right to dissent from some activities and pronouncements, the majority contended that member churches inherently were corporately responsible for what the WCC said and did in the name of the member churches. The detailed and specific statements of the council on social, economic, and political issues were from the Reformed point of view improper intrusions into the nonchurch areas of life.[7]

Finally, the implications of membership represented an insurmountable barrier for the majority. Simply by joining, a genuinely Reformed church would inevitably have to endorse the inclusive methodology of the WCC, recognize all member churches as churches of Christ, and as a con-

---

7. All ecumenical organizations make pronouncements on ethical, social, political, and economic issues. The RES (Chicago, 1984) issued a "Call to Commitment and Action" and a "Testimony on Human Rights." The same synod made several specific pronouncements for its member churches. For example:

> "We reaffirm our commitment to the task of the church in its preaching, teaching, pastoral, diaconal, and fellowshipping ministries to be a vital and vigorous advocate and practitioner of a biblical view of human rights as a crucial aspect of its calling to equip the Christian community for its witness in the world. . . .
> "We urge our member churches, especially those in North America and Europe, in cooperation with our member churches in Latin America, to do all in their power to help alleviate the widespread and atrocious violations of human rights which have been inflicted upon the severely suffering Latin American peoples." (Quoted in *Agenda for Synod, 1986*, p. 191)

sequence relativize and confuse its own Reformed witness. A church inescapably compromised its confessional standards and integrity if it became a member. Recalling the earlier opinion of the Committee on Ecumenicity and Church Correspondence — that nonmembership, when properly expressed and for good reasons, was more vocal than membership in a large organization — the majority said that nonmembership offered the possibility of a clear witness and should be chosen in preference to membership in this council. For the reasons indicated, the majority concluded that membership in the WCC could not be considered a permissible course of action for a Reformed church in discharging its ecumenical responsibilities.

The point of departure and primary concern for the minority was the inescapable ecumenical calling and responsibility given the church by Christ. The CRC, the minority said, had recognized this calling, particularly in the ecumenical vision expressed in the report of 1944, but it did not yet have a concrete avenue through which to approach a large portion of Christ's church. The WCC now offered itself as such an avenue. The question therefore confronting the CRC was whether or not this council could be used as one means for fulfilling its ecumenical calling. The minority first presented the World Council's official position, quoting the basis and portions of the Toronto Statement.[8] They then raised the question whether or not

8. An abbreviated statement was reproduced in the minority report to synod in 1967. It included:

a. The following negations:

1) The WCC is not and must never become a Super-church.

2) The purpose of the WCC is not to negotiate unions between churches, which can only be done by the churches themselves acting on their own initiative, but to bring the churches into living contact with each other and to promote the study and discussion of the issues of church unity.

3) The WCC cannot and should not be based on any one particular conception of the church. It does not prejudge the ecclesiastical problem.

71

membership in the WCC was permissible. If membership involved a denial of the Christian faith or abandonment of loyalty to either the Scriptures or the Reformed confessions, it obviously would not be permissible.

In response to questions raised regarding the adequacy of the basis, the minority judged that the basis was sufficient for the purpose for which it was intended. It

4) Membership in the WCC does not imply that a church treats its own conception of the church as merely relative.

5) Membership in the WCC does not imply the acceptance of a specific doctrine concerning the nature of church unity.

b. The following affirmations:

1) The member churches of the council believe that conversation, co-operation, and common witness of the churches must be based on the common recognition that Christ is the Divine Head of the Body.

2) The member churches of the WCC believe on the basis of the New Testament that the church of Christ is one.

3) The member churches recognize that the membership of the church of Christ is more inclusive than the membership of their own church body. They seek, therefore, to enter into living contact with those outside their own ranks who confess the Lordship of Christ.

4) The member churches of the WCC consider the relationship of other churches to the Holy Catholic Church which the creeds profess as a subject for mutual consideration. Nevertheless, membership does not imply that each church must regard the other member churches as churches in the true and full sense of the word.

5) The member churches of the WCC recognize in other churches elements of the true church. They consider that this mutual recognition obliges them to enter into serious conversation with each other in the hope that these elements of truth will lead to the full truth and to unity based on the full truth.

6) The member churches of the council are willing to consult together in seeking to learn of the Lord Jesus Christ what witness He would have them bear to the world in His Name.

7) A further practical implication of common membership in the WCC is that the member churches should recognize their solidarity with each other, render assistance to each other in case of need, and refrain from such actions as are incompatible with brotherly relationships.

8) The member churches enter into spiritual relationship through which they seek to learn from each other and to give help to each other in order that the Body of Christ may be built up and that the life of the churches may be renewed. (*Acts of Synod, 1967*, pp. 459-60)

expressed, although minimally, the unity of the church given in Christ and provided a limited platform for further growth toward unity. The basis, as it stood, was not adequate for a merger between churches or the kind of joint witness and action of confessional Reformed churches in an organization such as the RES. But it was sufficient to bring together, in a tentative way, all Christians for joint consultation and limited action, in keeping with the council's purpose.

Difficulties in recognizing other churches as churches, the minority thought, should not be a stumbling block to a Reformed church. Reformed churches should and do in fact give a measure of recognition to other churches, even those they severely criticize and with which they have basic differences. The World Council itself did not require member churches to acknowledge other churches as churches in the full sense of the word but only to recognize in them elements or vestiges of the church. All Christian churches, the minority said, respect the churchly character of other bodies by accepting as valid the baptism administered in them. The minority found remarkable agreement between the Toronto Statement and the report of 1944. While the statement and the report presented different ways of approaching other churches — the one by ecumenical organization, the other by church correspondence — both approaches were based on a common recognition that other churches were churches of Christ.

The minority also answered objections to membership in the World Council drawn from the implications of the council's claim to be a fellowship of churches. Church fellowships, the minority contended, were and should be variously defined. The CRC itself, for example, was a fellowship closely defined in doctrine, government, worship, and activities. The RES was a more loosely defined fellowship of churches, and the WCC a fellowship even more loosely defined. The minority judged that the fellowship described in the council's documents was a special kind of fellowship, very limited in nature and not yet very sharply defined. The consequences, however, of denying the WCC the right to claim even the very limited fellowship expressed in the official documents would be detrimental to the recognition of Christ's work in the numerous churches affiliated with the council.

Objections to the manner in which the basis was maintained and functioned in the World Council were answered by appealing to the nature and purpose of both the council and its basis. The WCC, the minority pointed out, was not itself a church but a fellowship of churches. Consequently it did not have authority to exercise discipline. The basis admittedly was less than a creed or confession. Its purpose was not to serve as a standard for orthodoxy but to indicate the nature of the fellowship and the orientation point for the work that it did. In the minority's opinion, the World Council, within the limited framework of its purpose, did take its basis seriously. It did not, however, officially interpret the basis, thus allowing member churches much greater freedom of interpretation of that basis than could be allowed of creeds and confessions within a confessional church.

Heresy in WCC member churches, the minority granted, was indeed the problem with membership for an orthodox church. The WCC, however, neither created nor accentuated the problem, though it did offer a meeting place where heresy could be confronted and addressed. The minority dismissed the burden of corporate responsibility for the council's objectionable public statements by asserting that no church was bound by any statement the council might make, certainly not by any that was in conflict with a member church's confessional position.[9] The problems

9. The Rules of the WCC regarding public statements includes the following: "While such statements may have great significance and influence as the expression of the judgment or concern of so widely representative a Christian body, yet their authority will consist only in the weight which they carry by their own truth and wisdom and the publishing of such statements shall not be held to imply that the World Council as such

confronting an orthodox church contemplating membership in the World Council, the minority thought, were not sufficient to warrant a refusal to join. In contrast to the majority, the minority concluded "that membership in the WCC does not constitute a denial of the faith nor involve a failure in obedience to the Word or loyalty to the Reformed confessions, and therefore must be judged permissible to a Reformed church."[10]

The majority did not wish to give the synod the impression that they were deficient in their ecumenical vision and sense of responsibility. After vigorously opposing membership in the WCC, the majority said that their attitude toward the WCC and its member churches was not wholly negative. The CRC had a responsibility to the world and to the churches of the world. The majority proposed, therefore, that the CRC actively pursue its ecumenical calling along the lines suggested in the report of 1944. A beginning should be made with such evangelical Protestant churches as the Lutheran Church–Missouri Synod and the Southern Baptists. Simultaneously, contacts should be established with other churches that had rejected the Protestant Reformation — the Roman Catholic Church, and even the Eastern Orthodox Church. As far as procedure to be followed in making these contacts was concerned, the majority had no more to say than the study committee in 1944. They simply said that they did not dare to say how such contacts could be legitimately and judiciously pursued. Special committees, they suggested, should be appointed to study the many challenging facets of the church's great ecumenical responsibility.

While endorsing the breadth of the ecumenical vision of the report of 1944, the majority did not express itself in

---

has, or can have, any constitutional authority over the constituent churches or right to speak for them." Quoted in Minority Report, *Acts of Synod, 1967*, pp. 460-61.

10. *Acts of Synod, 1967*, p. 474.

the same tone and manner as did the earlier report. Nor did they as clearly state the purpose of contacts with other churches. As a matter of fact, the majority never explained what the ecumenical task and responsibility of the CRC was.

In the concluding section of their report, the minority wrestled with the question of whether or not membership in the WCC was advisable for the CRC. In the minority's opinion the question was simply a matter of strategy or tactics. The World Council offered undeniable opportunities for ecumenical contact not available to the CRC in any other organization. The minority also thought it was the only viable means for carrying out the church's ecumenical responsibility to all of Christ's churches. Nevertheless, they were profoundly aware of serious difficulties and problems with membership in the WCC. The ecclesiastical character and the specific nature of the fellowship of the WCC remained fraught with ambiguities and uncertainties. The doctrinal content of the basis was extremely limited and allowed a wide range of theological interpretation. The fact that it did not commit the council to a more definite interpretation of Scripture, the minority believed, confronted the CRC with serious difficulties. The minority doubted that the church's yearning after fellowship and witness in an arena as large and complex as the World Council was sufficient to warrant the effort to cope with these difficulties. The minority was also uncertain about some of the present trends within the council; it seemed bent, for instance, on making greater claims regarding its own ecclesiastical character, and some voices within the council seemed to be syncretistically undermining the absolute distinction between Christianity and the non-Christian religions. More information was needed to sort out the uncertainties, and more time required to determine the trends.

Due to lingering difficulties and uncertainties, the lack of information on crucial matters, and the CRC's lack of ecumenical experience, the minority judged that the church was not ready to enter the ecumenical arena of the WCC.

Pastoral sensitivities also played a significant role in the minority's advice to synod to postpone a decision on membership. The church's closest circle of fellowship was within the denomination; the intimacy of this fellowship, the minority said, should not be disrupted or even jeopardized by experimenting with a wider undertaking in unity.

Before presenting its recommendations regarding membership in the WCC and its advice to the GKN, the synodical advisory committee presented a list of statements intended to provide the proper context for understanding its recommendations. The statements indicate the committee's concern to affirm the catholicity of the church and to set forth the scope of the CRC's ecumenical responsibility. They also assert the necessity of separation for the truth of the gospel. The list included the following:

- that there is only one church of Jesus Christ and that the church's unity should come to visible expression;

- that the Christian Reformed Church has a responsibility with respect to all Christian churches;

- that we want to obey the Lord, both in seeking fellowship with all those who confess Jesus Christ, and in separating ourselves from those who reject, deny, or pervert the truth of the Gospel.[11]

The opening debate, beginning at 7:30 p.m. and lasting until after midnight, was intense. Feelings came powerfully to the surface and some interpersonal relations were badly frayed. The next morning the synod adopted a series of recommendations on membership in the WCC that in substance represented the position of the majority report.[12]

11. *Acts of Synod, 1967*, p. 89.
12. The main recommendation was the following:

Although fully aware of the ecumenical calling of Christ's church as expressed in the synodical report of 1944 . . . , and therefore of the responsibility to contact all those churches in which some traces of the catholic church of Jesus Christ are still to be found, synod declares with

In response to the GKN's resolution, the synod judged that in view of the grave implications of membership, to state that there was "no decisive impediment" to it was not sufficient. Membership required a convincing demonstration of obedience to Scripture. The synod also made two requests of the GKN: (1) To make their contribution in working out a positive statement of the Reformed churches' ecumenical calling in the context of Articles 27–29 of the Belgic Confession, and (2) to bear in mind the ecclesiastical situation and environment in North America where Reformed churches were confronted by theological modernism and where evangelical churches generally were opposed to the WCC. Finally, the synod reminded the GKN that joining the WCC meant giving recognition to churches with a radically different interpretation of the gospel. Membership in the council, even if permissible, the synod said, would be inadvisable. These decisions, together with the majority and minority reports of the study committee, were forwarded to the GKN. After the meeting of the RES held in Amsterdam in 1968, the GKN became a member of the WCC.

Since 1967 no serious discussion or consideration of membership in the WCC has taken place in the CRC. Individual members of the CRC have made noteworthy contributions to the work of the council. Dr. Stuart Kingma was for many years the Director of the Christian Medical Commission and Marlin Van Elderen is presently editor of *One World*, the monthly magazine of the WCC.[13]

---

regret that it is not permissible for the Christian Reformed Church to join the fellowship of the World Council of Churches because of its present nature, its inadequate basis, the maintenance and functioning of that basis, its socio-political activities and declarations, and the implications of membership in this council. (*Acts of Synod, 1967*, p. 89)

13. For another discussion of the CRC and the WCC, see Klaas Runia, "The Christian Reformed Church and the World Council of Churches," in *Perspectives on the Christian Reformed Church,* ed. Peter De Klerk and Richard R. De Ridder (Grand Rapids: Baker Book House), pp. 325-43.

The Crisis in the Reformed Ecumenical Synod

Although the RES has never occupied a very prominent place in the minds and hearts of CRC members, the church has officially through its synod, the Interchurch Relations Committee, and delegates to Reformed ecumenical synods given the RES strong, consistent, and loyal support.

At the 1968 meeting of the RES in Amsterdam, it became apparent that strict confessional Reformed ecumenicity had entered murky and troubled waters. Delegates from the CRC reported that the meetings were marked by tension, and that if present trends continued the RES faced a growing crisis in the years ahead. At the request of the GKN, whose delegates had already experienced considerable difficulty in interactions with delegates from other churches at the 1963 meetings in Grand Rapids, the Amsterdam synod issued a statement asking the member churches to embrace one another in mutual trust and to show sympathy for one another's problems and patience with one another's weaknesses. During the last two decades the tensions within the synod have increased. Developments within the GKN and race relations in South Africa and among the South African member churches occasioned and have sustained the crisis.

The GKN was one of the original partners in founding the RES; it is also the "mother church" of the majority of the Reformed member churches of the synod. As the second largest member body, with approximately 800,000 members, and in its historical position of leadership in Reformed theology and Calvinism among conservative Reformed churches and communities worldwide, the GKN is a formative and influential force in the ecumenical synod. The fact that the GKN joined the WCC, even though every assembly of the RES since Edinburgh in 1953 had advised against membership, had very serious repercussions among some of the member churches.[14] Before the 1972 meeting of the RES in

14. Two Indonesian daughter churches of the GKN are also mem-

Australia, the Orthodox Presbyterian Church (OPC) sent letters to all member churches, calling into question the creedal commitment of the GKN and asking the synod to decide whether or not it could rightfully maintain membership in the synod. The letter specifically mentioned five items: membership in the WCC, the admission of women to the teaching and ruling offices in the church, the repeal of the decisions of the Synod of Assen in 1926 that affirmed a literal interpretation of Genesis 2 and 3, the doctrine of Scripture held in the GKN, and, more recently, failure to administer discipline in response to Dr. H. M. Kuitert's questioning of the historicity of the fall of man. "Homophilical Members of the Congregation," the pastoral advice approved by the general synod of the GKN in 1979 that permitted homosexual relationships on the part of church members and officeholders, has served to intensify the crisis. At every gathering of the RES since 1972 member churches have requested that the membership of the GKN be terminated, but no such motion has received a majority vote.

The synods have, however, spoken with increasing directness to the GKN on the issues and to the crisis that the GKN's positions and practices have precipitated within the fellowship. While acknowledging the problems confronting the GKN in disciplining its theologians and officeholders, the Synod of Cape Town stated that if these problems were given a higher priority than the duty of the church to protect the people of God from apostasy, then the GKN would lose the marks of the true church. The

---

bers of both the RES and the WCC. Every gathering of the RES since Edinburgh in 1953 has had on its agenda the question of dual membership in the RES and the WCC. Reformed ecumenical synods, including the most recent at Harare, Zimbabwe, in 1988, have advised against membership in the World Council. The Synod of Cape Town in 1976, in addition to reaffirming the advice, expressly declared that membership in the WCC was inconsistent with membership in the RES. The RES now tolerates dual membership. The most recent synod decided not to terminate the membership of an RES member church solely on account of its joining the World Council.

synod further reminded the GKN that a policy that permitted unbiblical teaching and practice in the church was a violation of the Constitution of the RES. Similarly, the Synod of Chicago in 1984 expressed its most urgent concern about the crisis in the fellowship of the RES occasioned by the GKN's practice of allowing even officeholders to engage in homosexual relationships. The synod asked the GKN to withdraw its statement of pastoral advice. If it was unable to do so, the synod cautioned, several member churches would find it difficult to stay in the RES.

General synods of the GKN have regularly had on their agenda the question whether or not to remain a member of the RES. To date the church has decided, in spite of the persistent opposition, to remain with the synod.[15] During the last twenty years of crisis, nine churches have resigned their membership, allegedly because of the serious defects in Reformed faith and practice present in the GKN and because of the continued presence of this church in the fellowship of the RES.

Although somewhat less threatening to the existence of the RES, the racial tensions in South Africa have contributed to the mounting crisis within the organization. The racial attitudes and practices of the white Reformed churches in South Africa have created tensions between them and Reformed churches outside South Africa, especially the GKN. Increasingly, racial problems in South Africa have become a source of irritation and conflict between South African member churches. Already at the synod in Potchefstroom, South Africa, in 1958, the RES adopted a "Report on Race Relations." After intense debate, race res-

15. The general synod of the GKN, meeting after the RES at Harare in 1988, decided by a vote of 37 out of 73 delegates to remain members of the Reformed Ecumenical Council (REC). The Harare synod changed the name of the ecumenical gathering from a synod to a council. The change does not alter the constitution or purposes of the organization. The CRC originally proposed a council rather than a synod and in recent years recommended the change.

olutions were again adopted at the Reformed ecumenical synods of Amsterdam (1968) and of Australia (1972).

The riots in Soweto in June 1976 and intermittent ones elsewhere — including those in Cape Town prior to and during the meetings of the RES there in August — provided the context for race relations to be urgently addressed. The synod revised earlier race resolutions, adopted new ones that specifically addressed the escalating unrest and the reasons for it, sent a delegation to Prime Minister Vorster, and put an interpretive commission in place. This commission was asked, on the one hand, to interpret the insights and experience of the worldwide Reformed community to their South African fellow members, and on the other, to interpret the attitudes and actions of the South African churches to their Reformed fellow members throughout the world.

The commission's report, "South African Race Relations," was submitted to the Synod of Nimes in 1980. In the judgment of the CRC delegation the report produced little fruitful discussion. The basic questions concerning the South African policy called "apartheid" or separate development were sidetracked. The fact that Dr. Allan Boesak of the racially mixed (coloured) Dutch Reformed Mission Church (DRMC) and the Rev. Sam Buti of the black Dutch Reformed Church in Africa (DRCA) boycotted the meeting at which the commission's report was discussed contributed to the synod's failure to come to grips with the issue. Boesak and Buti felt that discussing apartheid at Nimes would be an exercise in futility. Their absence, however, underscored the underlying tension within the South African member churches.

In 1982 the DRMC and the World Alliance of Reformed Churches (WARC) issued a declaration on apartheid. Both the church and the alliance stated that the moral and theological justification of apartheid constituted a *status confessionis* — that is, a matter of concern about which it is impossible to differ without affecting the integrity of the communal confession of the Reformed churches. Both bodies further declared that apartheid was a sin and that its moral and theological justification was a heresy. Prior to the meeting of the RES in Chicago (1984), the DRMC requested responses from the member churches to its statement and asked that these responses be forwarded to the synod for consideration and possible action. Since the issue as presented touched on Reformed confessional integrity and might have serious implications, especially for the white South African churches and their continued membership in the RES, the Chicago synod debated the matter intensely. After a long discussion, a series of recommendations addressed to the South African churches was adopted. The decision included the following statement:

> That synod declare that, when the evil of such an ideology has been exposed from within the church itself and the church(es) nevertheless would continue to support or fail to denounce such an ideology, there is a *Status Confessionis*. This means that this particular matter has then become a point of confession about which one cannot differ without affecting the integrity of the entire Christian confession. In such a situation any teaching of the church that would defend this ideology would have to be regarded as heretical, i.e., in conflict with the teaching of Scripture.[16]

Not long after the Synod of Chicago, the executive committee of the Dutch Reformed Church in South Africa (DRC), the largest member body of the RES, suspended its RES membership. Two reasons were given for the action: the continued presence of the GKN in the synod and the decisions on race adopted in Chicago. These decisions on race, in the judgment of the executive committee, were contrary to the stipulations of the RES Constitution. The crisis in the RES had deepened. The general synod of the DRC in 1986 decided to lift the suspension and to remain

16. Quoted in *Acts of Synod, 1985*, p. 213.

in the RES. Although a majority of the synodical delegates favored the recommendation of the executive committee to terminate membership, the motion failed because it did not receive the required two-thirds majority.

During these decades of crisis, CRC synods and delegates to Reformed ecumenical synods have made diligent efforts, within the legitimate boundaries of the church's Reformed faith and conscience, to preserve the RES and to enhance its effectiveness. The RES is the only international ecumenical organization with which the church is affiliated, and it does not want the synod either to disintegrate or to be reduced to insignificance. There are, however, more fundamental reasons for the church's efforts to maintain the synod. The CRC believes it has a responsibility to all the confessional Reformed churches in the world and owes them its fellowship. The RES has been the meeting place for exercising this responsibility and for participating in this fellowship. Consequently, preserving the RES has been for the CRC a matter of priority and concern.

The CRC has been a mediating and moderating influence within the synod, often leaving the leadership to others. Without accommodating itself to doctrinal and ethical error, the CRC, both by synodical decisions and by the advice of the Interchurch Relations Committee, has resisted efforts to expel or force the termination of the GKN's membership in the synod. Rather than using the RES as an arena for criticizing and rebuking the GKN, the CRC has spoken directly to the GKN through its synod and interchurch committee.

Whether or not the CRC has been as evenhanded on South African racial issues within the RES might be disputed. To date, however, the church has not called for the termination of the membership of any of the South African churches, nor has it threatened to withdraw its membership on account of racial attitudes present within South African Reformed churches. It has, however, as a matter of conscience, addressed itself to the South African situation and apartheid. The Interchurch Relations Committee, in a letter to the Cape Town synod, recommended the appointment of an interpretive commission. The synod agreed with the recommendation and appointed one. The CRC also adopted a statement on apartheid as an ideology and in it judged that a theological defense of this ideology is, indeed, a heresy.

The North American Presbyterian and Reformed Council

The Presbyterian Church in America (PCA), a secession movement out of the Presbyterian Church in the U.S. (Southern), was organized in 1973. Early the next year this new denomination called a meeting of representatives from the North American Reformed churches generally recognized as seriously committed to both the letter and spirit of their confessional standards. The Christian Reformed Church, the Orthodox Presbyterian Church, the Reformed Presbyterian Church (Evangelical Synod), and the Reformed Presbyterian Church in North America were invited and sent representatives. At the meeting the unity of the church and organic union as a viable goal were discussed. The representatives were sufficiently encouraged by their conversation to call a plenary session of representatives of the interchurch relations committees from their respective churches to discuss closer relationships. The meeting was held late in October 1974 in Pittsburgh. The outcome of the meeting was considerably less than a proposal for an organic union of the churches. At this meeting, however, a council of churches, the North American Presbyterian and Reformed Council (NAPARC), was organized.

The new council's Statement of Basis affirmed a commitment to Jesus Christ as only Savior and sovereign Lord over all of life. It further stated that the fellowship of the participating churches was based on a full commitment both to the Scriptures as the infallible Word of God and to their teachings as set forth in the Reformed confessional standards. A common commitment to Scripture and the Reformed standards was to be regarded as a warrant for advising, counseling, and cooperating with one another and as a basis for holding out before each other the desirability and need for the organic union of churches that were of like faith and practice. Although secondary to the formation of the council, catholicity and organic union were clearly part of the original vision and purpose. The synod of the CRC in 1975 had no difficulty formalizing its membership in the council on the basis and for the purposes proposed. Later, the Associate Reformed Presbyterian Church and the Korean American Presbyterian Church joined the other four charter members and are now also members of NAPARC. Presently, the Evangelical Presbyterian Church (EPC), a secession movement organized in 1981 out of the United Presbyterian Church in the U.S.A., is applying for membership in the council.[17]

NAPARC has become the principal ecumenical instrument through which the CRC meets its ecumenical calling to and expresses its unity with other North American Reformed churches. The council has worked very much to the satisfaction of the CRC.[18] The NAPARC churches have en-

17. The EPC seceded for reasons of doctrine and church polity. The doctrinal issue was admitting to the ministry a candidate who refused to affirm belief in the deity of Jesus Christ. Making the election of women to the office of elder mandatory for all congregations was the polity matter. The congregations of the EPC did not enter one of the already existing Presbyterian groups because they were convinced that less essential theological matters would bar their acceptance. The EPC has as its motto: "In essentials unity, in nonessentials liberty, in all things charity." In keeping with its motto, the EPC permits local congregations to decide whether or not women may serve in church offices. The EPC is a member both of WARC and the NAE.

18. This judgment may in the near future have to be revised. Upon the recommendation of the Commission on Ecumenicity and Interchurch

gaged in cooperative studies and have mutually endorsed a "Golden Rule" comity agreement for church planting and an agreement on transfer of members and congregations. They have also expressed their unity in Christ by holding concurrent synods on the campus of Calvin College and Seminary in Grand Rapids, Michigan. Representatives of the denominational agencies of the member churches meet regularly to share insights and to promote cooperation. The original goal of organic union has not been entirely lost. The PCA invited the Reformed Presbyterian Church (Evangelical Synod) and the OPC to discuss church union. Both churches accepted the invitation. The Reformed Presbyterian group has now entered into the fellowship of the PCA. Efforts to bring the OPC and the PCA together have thus far not succeeded. The CRC has neither invited other NAPARC churches nor been invited by them to discuss organic union.

Deteriorating Relationships with Old Sisters

The CRC and GKN

Beginning in 1969 a process was set in motion that has resulted in reducing the degree of ecclesiastical intimacy between the CRC and its oldest and formerly closest sister, the GKN. That year the synod instructed its Interchurch Relations Committee to consider whether the changes occurring in its sister church warranted a change in the relationship between the churches. The following year the com-

---

Relations of the OPC, NAPARC at its November 8, 1990, meeting voted unanimously (the CRC delegation not voting) to "call upon the Christian Reformed Church to reverse the action of the 1990 synod leading to the opening of the offices of minister and ruling elder to women, as contrary to the Scripture and the Reformed standards. . . ." (*Agenda for Synod, 1991,* pp. 164 and 533).

mittee reported that it had serious reservations concerning reported developments in the GKN. The reservations concerned doctrinal deviations, stemming from the use of the new hermeneutic, that were now seemingly condoned in that church. Upon the recommendation of its interchurch committee, the synod addressed a letter of admonition to the GKN in the spirit of a concerned sister. The synod received a cordial letter in response, but it came too late for synodical action in 1972. The letter stated that the churches in the Netherlands, in accordance with the Belgic Confession, affirmed the authority of Scripture, based on its contents. The letter also said that ignoring the authority of the confessions leads to ignoring the authority of the Bible.

The failure of the GKN, however, to follow through with church discipline in the manner that some congregations in the CRC thought necessary continued to render a sister-church relationship problematic. As historically understood in the Reformed tradition, sister churches were one in doctrine and practice, and were it not for barriers of geographical distance and differences in language, they would unite in one organization. In view of the deviations in the GKN and its failure to apply discipline in the manner thought necessary, some Christian Reformed congregations no longer believed the two churches were essentially one in doctrine and life. Therefore, they requested that the sister-church relationship with the GKN be terminated. Recognizing the difficulties involved in working with the sister-church concept — not only with respect to the GKN but with other churches as well — the Interchurch Relations Committee asked the synod for permission to review and possibly redefine its system of correspondence. The committee said it desired a new system for classifying churches that would take into consideration the realities of the church's present ecclesiastical situation worldwide, insure adequate safeguards for the CRC's doctrinal integrity, and enable it to work fully and freely for the unity of the church of Jesus Christ without detracting from its commitment to the truth of Scripture and the teaching of the confessions. The synod complied with the request.

In 1974 the synod approved a recommendation from the interchurch committee to abandon the old twofold classification of sister churches and churches in correspondence and to replace it with a single category called "Churches in Ecclesiastical Fellowship." The specific terms of the interchurch fellowship as adopted by synod were the following:

> a. exchange of fraternal delegates at major assemblies,
> b. occasional pulpit fellowship,
> c. intercommunion (i.e., fellowship at the table of the Lord),
> d. joint action in areas of common responsibility,
> e. communication on major issues of joint concern,
> f. the exercise of mutual concern and admonition with a view to promoting the fundamentals of Christian unity.[19]

This new classification is both broader and less intimate than the older sister-church relationship. The essential elements of the former classifications, however, remain unchanged. The new system also allows for more flexibility

19. *Acts of Synod, 1974,* p. 57. At present the CRC maintains a relationship of ecclesiastical fellowship with twenty-three churches. They are the Associate Reformed Presbyterian Church, Christian Church of Sumba, Christian Reformed Church of Nigeria, Christian Reformed Churches in the Netherlands, Church of Christ in the Sudan among the TIV, Dutch Reformed Church in Africa, Dutch Reformed Church in Sri Lanka, Dutch Reformed Mission Church, Evangelical Presbyterian Church, Evangelical Reformed Church of Brazil, Korean American Presbyterian Church, Netherlands Reformed Churches, Orthodox Presbyterian Church, Presbyterian Church in America, Reformed Church in Africa, Reformed Church in America, Reformed Church in Argentina, Reformed Church in Japan, Reformed Churches in Australia, Reformed Churches in New Zealand, Reformed Churches in South Africa, Reformed Churches in South Africa (Synod Soutpansberg), Reformed Churches in South Africa (Synod Midlands), Reformed Churches in the Netherlands, and Reformed Presbyterian Church in North America.

because the terms of fellowship and cooperation with individual churches can be specifically determined and in some cases limited. This flexibility permits the CRC to continue to assist, encourage, and admonish other Reformed churches with whose doctrine and practice it does not fully agree without terminating its interchurch relationship or compromising its own Reformed integrity.

While the new system relieved the pressure within the CRC to sever its long-standing relationship with the GKN, the concern over developments within that denomination remained. Christian Reformed fraternal delegates to the general synods of the GKN openly criticized them for their hesitant and vacillating approach to church discipline. Their reluctance suggested to the CRC that they were more concerned to preserve unity in a structural sense than to preserve unity in the truth.

Two actions of the general Synod of Delft (1979–80) especially heightened concern in the CRC regarding the GKN's purity in life and doctrine. The first was the statement of pastoral advice, "Homophilical Members of the Congregation"; the second was the endorsement of a report on the nature of biblical authority issued by the GKN's Deputies on Church and Theology, entitled "God With Us." Already in 1980 the synod of the CRC expressed its alarm that the Synod of Delft had seemingly spoken with approval of homosexual expression (*beleven*). The synod of the CRC instructed its interchurch committee to seek further clarification of the language and implications of Delft's decision and to reexamine the present provisions for table and pulpit fellowship between the two churches. In 1981 the synod instructed the committee to study the report "God With Us," and to look especially into the report's implications for continued interchurch fellowship.

The GKN sent a letter of clarification and two fraternal delegates to the synod of the CRC in 1981 in order to help the CRC understand the statement of pastoral advice. The letter and delegates explained the circumstances and content of the statement and reaffirmed the unqualified right of homosexual church members to remain in good standing regardless of their sexual disposition and experience. The letter also critically examined the CRC's statement on homosexuality adopted in 1973. The 1973 report had made a distinction between homosexual disposition or orientation and homosexual practice. The practice, it said, was sinful. The GKN not only denied the propriety of the distinction but also judged that overt homosexual activity and behavior were not always or necessarily sinful. While expressing appreciation for the GKN's willingness to clarify its position and to deal pastorally with homophilical members, the synod in 1981 stated that it did not believe the GKN's course of action was either wise or biblical. What especially disturbed the synod was that the GKN allowed practicing homosexuals to hold office in the church. This openness, the synod believed, was clearly contrary to the Word of God. Therefore, the synod once again formally requested the GKN to reconsider, in the light of Scripture, its "extremely controversial and regrettable statement." It further asked the interchurch committee to advise the 1983 synod regarding continued table and pulpit fellowship with the church in the Netherlands. In 1983 the synod decided to redefine the terms of ecclesiastical fellowship with the GKN by withholding pulpit and table fellowship, except at the discretion of local consistories.

Subsequent to these decisions CRC fraternal delegates to general synods of the GKN have reported that the impact of the decisions has been keenly felt both by the synod and by the church's Committee of Deputies for Ecumenicity. While the deputies could understand the action of the CRC, they sincerely regretted its unilateral character. According to the fraternal delegates, the deputies deeply appreciated continued relations with the CRC and volunteered the conviction that "no one" in the GKN would support an effort to break or weaken the relationship between the two churches.

Since 1983 the GKN and its Committee of Deputies

for Ecumenicity have urged an intensification of discussions on matters of common concern between the churches. At the request of the church in the Netherlands, Professors Fred Klooster and John Stek from Calvin Seminary met with the Deputies for Church and Theology to discuss and critically review the report "God With Us." The GKN also sent Dr. J. Bakker and Professor C. Schippers to visit Christian Reformed churches and classes in Canada and the United States to interpret and explain the situation in which the GKN finds itself and its recent synodical decisions. These activities on the part of the GKN indicate very clearly the value it attaches to a continued relationship with the CRC. In spite of the firmness with which the CRC has spoken to the GKN, the church in the Netherlands has graciously expressed appreciation for the way the CRC conducts its interchurch relations.

The CRC and RCSA

Since 1980, the CRC's relationship with the Reformed Church in South Africa[20] has likewise come under ever-increasing scrutiny. This sister-church relationship is now in serious jeopardy. The South African church's official position on race relations, its practice in racial matters, and its failure to speak out vigorously against apartheid and the evils resulting from it comprise the source of the difficulty.[21] In 1982 the synod of the CRC declined a request from the DRC in South Africa for a relationship of ecclesiastical fel-

20. Official correspondence with this church dates back to 1866.

21. Although the two churches have a common origin, their historical development has not been quite the same. The CRC is today more inclined to address itself to social and political matters than is its South African counterpart. The South African church has persistently refused to make a declaration on apartheid as a social and political ideology and system on the ground that the church should deal with churchly matters only and not enter the social and political arenas.

lowship because of the DRC's official position on race. In the judgment of the CRC, entering a relationship of ecclesiastical fellowship with the DRC would seriously compromise its witness against racial discrimination and would suggest an attitude of indifference to the plight of millions of nonwhite South Africans, many of whom are Reformed Christians. The synod committed itself to reconsider the request after the DRC demonstrated genuine concern and action to undo both the system and the evils of apartheid.[22] The same synod asked the Interchurch Relations Committee to examine critically the position of the RCSA regarding race in order to determine whether or not that church should remain a church in ecclesiastical fellowship.

In 1983 the synod of the CRC was asked to sever ties with the RCSA. In response the synod mandated its interchurch committee to correspond with the church in South Africa regarding its official resolutions on race and its general practice in race relations. The synod also expressed its deep grief and distress over the unbiblical ideology and persistent practice of apartheid both in South African society and in the churches there. In 1984 the synod adopted the statement on apartheid and heresy. The following year the synod, in the light of a review of the most recent decisions of the RCSA adopted in January 1985, decided to inform the South African church that the relationship of ecclesiastical fellowship between the two churches was in grave danger. Behind this action was the synod's judgment that the decisions adopted in January continued to contain implicit theological support for apartheid. The synod further stated that the Scriptures demand that the RCSA repent of its sins against people of other

22. In 1990 the DRC adopted a completely revised edition of its testimony on race relations entitled "Church and Society." In this revised edition the large, white Afrikaner church for the first time officially rejected apartheid systems as sin. If the DRC's newly adopted position is as substantive as reported, the CRC and the DRC may soon enter a relationship of ecclesiastical fellowship.

races, bring its position and practice into conformity with the clear will of God, and seek racial justice and equality in South Africa. The synod did not, however, want to act precipitously in such an important matter. Since the South African church meets in general synod only once every three years, the synod decided to maintain the ties of fellowship until 1989, at which time the relationship between the churches would be reevaluated.

In 1985 the synod had also appointed a special committee of four — two representatives from the Interchurch Relations Committee and two from the Synodical Committee on Race Relations — to continue the dialogue with the RCSA. In 1986 the synod expressed frustration at the slow pace of the discussions and, entirely at its own initiative, asked the interchurch committee to insure that the South African church recognize that without meaningful change it would be almost impossible to maintain ecclesiastical fellowship between the churches after 1989. Once again, in 1987, apart from any committee recommendation, the synod reiterated its position, unequivocally rejecting apartheid as a gross violation of biblical principles and a repudiation of Christian ethical imperatives. By failing to lead its congregations and members in actively seeking justice and equality as is fitting of those who know the Lord and his Word, the synod said that the RCSA perpetuates and deepens division in the body of Christ, thus violating the unity of Christ. And once again in language that has become familiar, the synod expressed its grief that, without substantial and meaningful change, ecclesiastical fellowship after 1989 would be impossible.

The Synod of 1989 stopped short of terminating ecclesiastical fellowship with the RCSA. Instead, the synod decided to suspend fellowship with the white South African church until 1992. Very specific conditions were stated for lifting the suspension. The RCSA must (1) declare that apartheid is a sin and its theological defense is heretical, (2) give evidence of repentance for its complicity in the support of apartheid in

South Africa and the evils apartheid has created, and (3) publicly express its opposition to the system of apartheid and affirm its support of racial equality and justice for all peoples. Meanwhile, the Interchurch Relations Committee is to continue the dialogue with the RCSA and to submit to the Synod of 1992 a recommendation for either restoring or terminating ecclesiastical fellowship with the RCSA.

Renewal and Intensification of Relations with the Reformed Church in America

While the CRC's relationship to its two oldest sisters has been subjected to considerable stress and strain, its relationship to the church from which it originally seceded has followed a more positive course. Contacts between the two churches have, however, been intermittent rather than sustained, and they have lacked intimacy and strong commitment. Local congregational or "grass-roots" engagement and interdenominational cooperation have characterized this experiment in ecumenicity rather than discussions at the denominational level specifically intended to explore the possibility of organic union between the two churches.

In 1950 the RCA declined to enter into an official relationship of correspondence with the CRC on its terms. Nevertheless, the two churches somewhat sporadically continued to exchange fraternal delegates at the synodical level. In an effort to achieve greater understanding of one another and to clarify the relationship between them, the interchurch committees of the two churches formed a joint contact committee.[23] The synods of both denominations in 1966 encouraged closer fellowship between the churches at the local level and urged the classes to exchange fraternal

23. The specific date for the formation of the committee is not easy to recover. The record suggests that it was sometime in 1962.

delegates. In 1968 the meetings of the joint committee were discontinued at the request of the RCA because church-merger discussions between the Presbyterian Church in the U.S. and the RCA had reached a critical juncture; the RCA did not want them to be complicated by conversations with the CRC. The proposed merger, however, did not receive the necessary support in the RCA. At the suggestion of the RCA, the previously interrupted conversations were resumed. The representatives of the two denominations agreed that interchurch activities at the grass-roots level were the best way to approach and pursue ecumenical relations.

Beginning in 1972, jointly sponsored conferences of delegates and observers from the two denominations were held in places where there was a concentration of congregations from both denominations. These conferences emphasized the specific goal of interdenominational unity rather than the ultimate goal of church union. In 1975 the synods of both churches designated Reformation Day Sunday as a day for denomination-wide pulpit exchange and joint worship. Participation was by local option and local arrangement. The practice has continued. In 1976 the RCA and the CRC officially entered a fraternal relationship which in essence corresponds to the CRC's designation of "churches in ecclesiastical fellowship."

After 1976, contacts between the denominations at the local and classical levels have broadened and deepened. Discussions of the joint committee, however, floundered from inaction rather than from any specific difficulties. The joint committee's conversations were reinstated in 1984 and have continued since. The working consensus of opinion within the joint committee has been that, while reunion of the two churches ought to be the ultimate goal under the unifying Lordship of Jesus Christ, merger discussions at this time would be premature and possibly detrimental to the conversations. The committee's work has focused on monitoring current areas of cooperation and promoting mutual contacts, especially at the grass-roots level. The committee is also discussing important matters of mutual interest and concern such as the current relationship of the two churches, the state of the churches in comparison with each other, and the churches' responsibility to one another in view of their common background, confessions, and past history. The committee is seeking answers to questions such as how closer fellowship, more beneficial cooperation, and, possibly, joint endeavors can be realized, and how past and present differences inhibit the unity of the two denominations. In 1989 the RCA and the CRC visibly and experientially expressed their unity as churches in ecclesiastical fellowship when the synods of the two churches met concurrently on the campus of Calvin College.

Catholicity with Truth through Dialogue

The New Ecumenical Charter

The Interchurch Relations Committee and synods of the CRC increasingly felt the need for a statement of biblical and ecumenical principles to guide the work of the committee and to give direction to synods when decisions had to be made regarding relations with other churches and ecumenical organizations. To meet this need the synod asked the Interchurch Relations Committee to prepare and propose an ecumenical charter. The charter was to define the kind(s) of ecumenical relations which the church was to pursue, the objectives to be sought in these relationships, and the manner in which they were to be carried out. In formulating the charter, the committee was requested to take into account biblical and confessional considerations, past synodical statements and actions, current ecumenical commitments of the denomination, and anticipated developments in ecumenicity. The end product was the Ecumenical Charter of the Christian Reformed Church in North America, first proposed in 1985 and adopted in 1987.

The charter is based on broad biblical perspectives and the specific teachings of such passages as John 17, I Corinthians 12, and Ephesians 4. The charter affirms the

98

doctrine of the one holy catholic and apostolic church as confessed in the ancient creeds and the Reformed standards. It also reflects the formative decisions on ecumenicity and interchurch relations of previous synods — for example, the report of 1944 and the decisions of 1974 and 1977 on churches in ecclesiastical fellowship. At the same time it makes adjustments in approach and emphasis as a result of what the church has learned through experience. The charter is a well-ordered and well-structured document moving from biblical principles for ecumenicity to the specific responsibilities of the Interchurch Relations Committee. Although the charter is brief, its scope is broad and its affirmation of ecumenical calling and responsibility is comprehensive.

The unity and catholicity of the church are treated in the first section presenting the biblical principles for ecumenicity. The church, the charter states, is called to testify to what it already is — spiritually one in Christ — but also to what it should still become — visibly one in Christ. To this unity the church is called: a unity in time and space as one worldwide church united with Christ its Head and with one another in its members. Church unity, the charter says, is already given in Christ. This given unity is also the basis and motivation for the unity that still escapes the church. In contrast to the report of 1944, the charter affirms the propriety of diversity in unity. This new feature of the charter is no doubt due to insights gained from the experience of ecumenical organizations that initially were so preoccupied with unity that they lost sight of the need and propriety of diversity. The new charter allows for diversity in worship, confessional formulas, and church order.

While still maintaining that the unity of the church must come to visible expression, the charter humbly acknowledges that the ideal form of such unity is yet unknown. In this judgment, too, the charter is chastened by the experience and insights of the modern ecumenical movement and assumes a position quite different from the report of 1944. In the earlier report the polity of the Reformed and Presbyterian churches was considered the scriptural system of church government and the only acceptable standard for a visibly united holy catholic church.

The charter emphatically asserts that the unity of the church of Christ is a unity in the truth. In elaborating this biblical principle, however, it introduces a new feature with far-reaching implications for implementing the church's ecumenical calling and responsibility. The report of 1944 assumed that the CRC was in doctrine the closest approximation of the scriptural norm for truth. Although humbly stated, this assumption, with the implicit superiority embodied in it, pretty much shaped the church's understanding of its ecumenical calling and determined its approach to other churches. In striking contrast, the charter states that en route to achieving unity a church must seek to overcome major differences in the perception of biblical truth, sharing its own perception as well as being open to those of others. The manner in which this is to be done is through ecumenical dialogue, a form of conversation through which it may be assumed God will teach all churches and perhaps unite them through a deeper common grasp of the truth. According to the charter, however, the mutual recognition of limited perceptions of the truth and the possibility of a deeper grasp of the truth through dialogue should not be understood in such a way as to undermine either the certainty of the truth already revealed and grasped or commitment to it. Applying these principles to the CRC, the charter explicitly states that as the CRC struggles for unity in the truth through dialogue, it does so fully committed to the Reformed faith and the confessions of the Reformed churches.

The second section of the charter dealing with the principles of ecumenical practice is divided into two parts: the first presents the principles for interchurch relations or the relation of one denomination to another; the second gives the principles for ecumenical organizations. With regard to the former the charter says the ecumenical task of the church arises from the fragmentation of the body of Christ. The unity of Christ's body calls the church to seek the reunion of denominations. The task does not, however, necessarily begin in working for the return of one church to another, nor in the union of one church with another. This principle, for the most part negatively stated and without further elaboration, leaves the beginning of the ecumenical task somewhat open-ended. Presumably, the principle learned from the CRC's previous ecumenical experience allows for, perhaps even recommends, the approach being followed in relating to the RCA. In the context of interchurch relations, the charter again comments on truth and perceptions of it. It says that in the search for unity the biblical message may not be compromised and that distorted perceptions of biblical truth that hinder the church's witness to Christ must be rejected. Yet since all perceptions of biblical truth are fallible and incomplete, the CRC must guard against the presumption that it possesses the truth in all its fullness. Dialogue also has an important role in interchurch relations. Through it churches can come to a deeper understanding of God's revelation and discover elements in the understanding of truth that reflect merely human and societal diversities.

Principles to guide the church in the area of ecumenical organizations are a new feature of the charter not included in the report of 1944. The charter states that the church in today's world must recognize that ecumenicity is being pursued through various types of ecumenical organizations. Through membership in these organizations a church may be able to carry out some aspects of its ecumenical responsibilities more efficiently than through interchurch relations. Membership in ecumenical organizations, the charter acknowledges, requires relationships of diverse kinds — probably meaning varying degrees of intimacy in ecclesiastical fellowship — consonant with the wide diversity of member churches within the organizations. The same principles used in interchurch relations — such as loyalty to the biblical message, and dialogue — must be employed by member churches in ecumenical organizations.

From biblical and ecumenical principles, the charter moves to the guidelines that must direct the CRC in carrying out its ecumenical task. Whereas the report of 1944 indiscriminately claimed a basis in biblical principles for its classification of churches and the setting of priorities in interchurch relations, the charter, recognizing the pragmatic and prudential character of these matters, places them in the context of guidelines. The charter and the earlier report are essentially in agreement in classifying churches. The charter classifies the churches of Christ into three groups representing ever-widening circles: Reformed churches, non-Reformed Protestant churches, and the Roman Catholic and Orthodox churches. The CRC should seek rapprochement, the charter says, with all churches of Christ but should give priority to Reformed churches, particularly to those that are not only Reformed historically and officially, but are also Reformed in practice.

Somewhat less emphatically than the report of 1944, the charter asserts that the unity of those churches that are Reformed in confession and practice should come to organizational expression as soon as possible. Chastened by the CRC's previous experience and the difficulties inherent in achieving organic unions, the charter realistically speaks of interim aims of rapprochement that should include the resolution of doctrinal differences if necessary, joint action where possible, and a common Reformed witness to the world. Beginning from this inner and more intimate circle of Reformed churches, the CRC, in seeking rapprochement with other churches of Christ, should then move out in ever-widening circles as circumstances and opportunities provide. In so doing it should make use of ecumenical organizations that enable it to carry out its ecumenical task more efficiently.

It remains to be seen how effectively the new charter

will serve the CRC in guiding and implementing its ecumenical calling. Its effectiveness is in no small measure contingent on how well it is understood in the church. Brevity is one of its virtues and strengths. If, however, its brevity contributes to misunderstanding, either of the principles themselves or of the application of them, this perceived strength could prove to be a weakness. A commentary on the charter could perhaps render it more understandable and enhance its immediate relevance to the ecumenical life of the church.

Reaffiliation with the
National Association of Evangelicals

In 1985, the same year the Ecumenical Charter was proposed, the Interchurch Relations Committee submitted to synod an extensive report on the World Alliance of Reformed Churches (WARC), together with a recommendation to accept an invitation to become a member of the alliance. The synod decided to postpone action on the invitation until after the synod had acted on the charter. In 1987 the interchurch committee presented to synod a report on the NAE and asked the synod to receive for information a recommendation to reaffiliate with the association. Therefore membership in both the WARC and the NAE was to be put on the agenda of the Synod of 1988. The churches were encouraged to study the reports and communicate their reactions to the two proposals.

The Interchurch Relations Committee recommended membership in the NAE as a legitimate avenue through which the CRC could at least partially fulfill its ecumenical calling within the broad spectrum of evangelical Christianity in America. Through the NAE's association with the World Evangelical Federation, membership would also provide the church with ecumenical contacts throughout the world. In recommending membership the committee emphasized both the positive contribution the CRC could conceivably make to the NAE and the benefits that could be derived from affiliation. The NAE, the committee said, would provide the CRC with an opportunity to witness to the Reformed faith and its implications for an all-embracing world-and-life view to the evangelical wing of American Christianity. The role and benefits of dialogue in ecumenical relations were likewise acknowledged. Since the NAE represented evangelical churches from a wide variety of traditions, theologies, and practices, it would provide the CRC an opportunity to be both strengthened in its own heritage and challenged by its encounter with other evangelicals. The possibility of participating with other evangelical Christians and churches in presenting a united voice on issues vital to other Christian bodies, secular America, and the United States government seemed attractive.

In arguing for membership the committee contended that nothing in the NAE's Statement of Faith would infringe upon the CRC's Reformed doctrinal integrity, nor would the program and practices of the NAE in any way compromise the church's Reformed character. The NAE was deliberately organized in such a way that any member church was free to participate and cooperate in the way it chose and to abstain from any activity it found objectionable. The earlier fears and objections to membership, the committee said, had been either corrected or proved unfounded. What criticisms remained were outweighed by the values of membership.

No objections to membership in the NAE were sent to the interchurch committee, and the synodical advisory committee unanimously supported membership. When the matter was presented to the synod for debate and decision, only one question was asked: How much would it cost? After that question was answered, the synod unanimously voted to reaffiliate with the NAE.

On the basis of a common evangelical faith rooted in

an infallible Bible, expressed in a commitment to the historical factuality of the New Testament apostolic witness to Christ, and reinforced by mutual opposition to Liberalism, the CRC joined an ecclesiastically ambiguous and theologically mixed association of church denominations, independent churches, Christian organizations, and individuals. While excluding liberals, the NAE now embraces in its membership Reformed and Arminian Christians and churches in approximately equal numbers. Holiness, Pentecostal, Mennonite, Baptist, Lutheran, Presbyterian, and Reformed churches comprise its diverse ecclesiastical spectrum. By joining, the CRC for the first time in almost forty years stepped out of its isolationist tradition and narrowly circumscribed ecumenical involvement exclusively with confessional Reformed churches. It did so recognizing that the NAE offered the only realistic means for ecumenical contact with a wide variety of American evangelical churches.

Membership in the World Alliance of Reformed Churches Rejected

In 1966 the CRC accepted an invitation to send an observer to the theological committee of what is now called the Caribbean and North American Area Council (CANAAC) of WARC, a practice that has continued ever since. In 1970 the church sent an observer delegate to the general council of WARC meeting in Nairobi, Kenya, and since then the church has sent observer delegates to general council meetings on a regular basis. Beginning in 1972 and annually since then, the CRC has delegated observers to the meetings of CANAAC. WARC and its regional council have very much appreciated the participation of the observer delegates and the contributions of Christian Reformed theologians to its theological committee. Frequently, representatives of the alliance have commented favorably on the exceptional competence of the church's theologians and observer delegates and on their remarkable knowledge of the classic Reformed tradition. Taking note of the fine contributions of representatives of the CRC to its theological committee and at its annual meetings during the past twelve years, CANAAC in 1984 cordially invited the CRC to become a member of WARC and the area council.

In 1985 the Interchurch Relations Committee recommended that the synod accept the invitation. Initially the committee supported its recommendation on the basis of the ecumenical vision articulated in the report of 1944. This report clearly affirmed an ecumenical responsibility, the committee said, to those Reformed churches that still were officially Reformed but had become delinquent in practice. With regret the committee observed that during the last forty years the CRC had done virtually nothing to meet its ecumenical calling to these historically Reformed churches.

After the Ecumenical Charter was adopted in 1987, the interchurch committee appealed to it as well as to the earlier report in presenting the case for membership. As a matter of principle the charter affirmed the propriety, necessity, and efficiency of ecumenical organizations for meeting ecumenical obligations. The committee further pointed out that ecumenical organizations were a prominent feature of modern church life. Rather than direct contacts between churches aimed at church unions, churches currently availed themselves of ecumenical organizations to express visibly their given unity in Christ. The committee also appealed to what the charter said regarding unity in truth and truth through dialogue. Applying these principles to the CRC's participation in an ecumenical organization such as WARC, the committee acknowledged that in struggling for unity in truth the church must be fully committed to the Reformed faith and its confessions. Yet at the same time, in seeking to overcome differences in the perception of biblical truth the church must not only share with others its perceptions; it must also be open to theirs. In ecumenical relationships, the committee said, the CRC must witness to the truth it confesses, but it must also humbly recognize that every church of Christ, as part of his body, gives evidence of the work of the Spirit of Christ within it.

The Interchurch Relations Committee did not defend the Reformed faith and practice of all of WARC's member churches. Some of the member churches, it admitted, were only broadly and generally Reformed and really quite internally defective in doctrine and the practice of church discipline. The committee instead approached the question of membership on the basis of the CRC's ecumenical calling and responsibility. In recommending membership in WARC as a legitimate avenue for fulfilling part of the church's ecumenical task, the committee made use of the classification of churches presented in the report of 1944 and in the charter. The committee identified Reformed churches that were not only historically Reformed but also Reformed in practice as "circle one" churches. "Circle two" churches were officially and historically Reformed but no longer so in practice. The Reformed churches of these different circles were therefore qualitatively different in the actualities of their ecclesiastical life — that is, in regard to the doctrine actually taught in them and in regard to discipline, as practiced or neglected. WARC, the committee said, contained within its membership churches from both circles one and two.

The committee moved formally beyond both the report of 1944 and the charter by suggesting that existing ecumenical organizations could be classified in the same manner as churches. The Reformed Ecumenical Synod (RES) and North American Presbyterian and Reformed Council (NAPARC) could thus be classified as circle-one ecumenical organizations and WARC as a circle-two ecumenical endeavor. From these distinctions, which the committee judged necessary, important inferences and conclusions were drawn. As a circle-two organization, WARC did not require of its member churches the same measure of commitment and fidelity to the Reformed confessions as did the circle-one organizations. WARC required only a general agreement to the historical Reformed confessions. Similarly WARC, as a circle-two organization, did not bind member churches to the same degree of corporate responsibility and obligation to assist one another in affirming and maintaining their biblical and confessional integrity. Nor did WARC assume a responsibility for terminating the membership of delinquent churches, as was the case in circle-one ecumenical organizations. On the basis of these distinctions and the conclusions drawn from them, the committee concluded that WARC's Statement of Basis was adequate for a circle-two ecumenical fellowship and that CRC membership in WARC did not render the church corporately responsible for defects in doctrine and life in other member churches. Nor did membership in any way compromise the CRC's Reformed witness and integrity.

In the committee's judgment, membership in WARC offered the CRC a feasible, positive avenue to fulfill its responsibility toward historically Reformed churches and new opportunities to carry out its ecumenical task in ever-widening circles of churches. It would enable the CRC to support and strengthen the Reformed witness of churches currently in the alliance that were also members of the RES, as well as others with which the CRC enjoyed a relationship of ecclesiastical fellowship. Membership would also afford the church new opportunities to encourage and help small, struggling Reformed churches throughout the world that were members of WARC. And finally, the committee said, WARC would provide the CRC an opportunity, through dialogue with member churches, to come to a deeper understanding of God's revelation. Anticipating that some would think that refusing to affiliate would present a stronger Reformed witness to the officially Reformed churches of circle two, the committee contended that non-affiliation might serve to reassure circle-one churches of the

108

CRC's Reformed character. Nonmembership, however, would not make a significant impression on circle-two churches. For meeting its ecumenical calling and responsibilities to historically but now defective Reformed churches, the CRC really had no other options or genuine alternative to WARC.

A few classes, churches, and individuals objected rather strenuously to membership in WARC. The most basic criticism was that membership would involve the CRC in an alliance — making common cause on an equal basis — with an organization that embraced within its membership several churches that were unashamedly liberal in their theological stance: the United Presbyterian Church in the U.S.A., the United Church of Christ, the United Church of Canada, and the Remonstrant Brotherhood in the Netherlands. An alliance with such churches, opponents of membership contended, was simply forbidden by the Word of God. Therefore membership would compromise, at the denominational level, what it means to be "Reformed."

By a vote of 90 to 82, the Synod of 1988 defeated the motion to accept the invitation to join WARC. Since the motion to join was simply defeated, no official reasons for the synod's decision were recorded. The synod's action indicates that the CRC was not ready to risk arousing uncertainty in its membership regarding its confessional distinctiveness and loyalty to the Reformed faith — a distinctiveness and loyalty historically maintained and secured through separation and isolation — by allowing its representatives to participate in ecumenical dialogue, on an equal basis, with those of other Reformed churches that were delinquent in doctrine and in discipline.

Conclusion:
Evaluation and Appraisal

The CRC became a separate ecclesiastical entity as a result of the secessions of 1834 and 1857. From them the church acquired not only its independent existence but also its most fundamental and distinctive features and characteristics. It was from the beginning evangelical and Reformed. The evangelicalism of the Secession of 1834 included a rather pronounced antipathy for religious Liberalism. From this early secession in the Netherlands, the CRC inherited a confessional Reformed orthodoxy and a strict pattern of Reformed government and discipline. The seceders considered the articles of faith expressed in the confessional standards of the Reformed churches in the Netherlands and the Church Order of Dort virtually synonymous with the teaching of Scripture. Where this doctrine, government, and discipline were present and practiced, they were confident the true church of Christ was present.

The letters of secession submitted to Classis Holland in 1857 clearly stated that the seceding congregations were separating from the RCA and from all other Protestant denominations in America. The letters also said they were returning to their former ecclesiastical standpoint. In the thinking of the secessionists, their action was not simply a matter of convenience or preference but one of ultimate loyalty to Christ and his Word. Because of the RCA's openness to and involvement with other Protestant churches in America, the secessionists were not sure that the RCA was the true church of Christ. They sincerely believed that only if they remained strictly faithful to the Reformed confessions and the church order of the historic Reformed churches in the Netherlands could they be certain that they still belonged to the true church. In their judgment, therefore, the secession was clearly for the sake of the truth and for the certainty of salvation.

In the wake of these two secession movements, the CRC developed a staunchly separatistic and isolationist mentality. Social cohesiveness, Reformed elitism, and a general attitude of superiority in matters pertaining to the church and theology came to characterize the CRC. A sharply delimited confessional Reformed consciousness and a sense of identity devoid of catholic Christian sensitivity — with the exception of awareness of continuity with the historic Reformed churches — became prominent elements in the church's self-understanding. Early, intermittent contacts with a few other confessional Reformed churches and church-union conversations in the decade of the 1890s did not quicken and expand the church's catholic sensitivities, but only reinforced its separateness and confirmed it in its isolation.

In 1898, after forty years of near isolation, a nascent catholic consciousness feebly expressed itself from deep within the bosom of the church. This early catholic awareness, however, was directed outward exclusively to other confessional Reformed churches that, like the CRC, maintained a strict pattern of discipline. That year the CRC introduced a program of official correspondence with other Reformed churches, primarily for the purpose of helping them keep foreign or non-Reformed elements out of their church life. The same synod expressed a desire for a worldwide synod or council of confessional Reformed churches. Distinctively Reformed considerations rather than genuinely catholic ones were the motivation. The purpose of the assembly, it was said, should be to assist churches in purging themselves of non-Reformed elements and to help one another in promoting soundly Reformed church life. Almost a half century later in 1946, the Reformed Ecumenical Synod, an undertaking in Reformed catholicity on a strict confessional basis, came into existence.

During the first half of the twentieth century, the anti-liberal component in the CRC's self-consciousness grew and eventually became an essential ingredient in its identity. The CRC had joined the Federal Council of Christian Churches in 1918 for purely pragmatic reasons — to place military chaplains. After the war, when the liberal stance and orientation of the council became strikingly apparent, the CRC quickly withdrew. At the time many in the church shared the general conviction of American Fundamentalists that any cooperation between liberals and orthodox Christians was contrary to the Word of God. In 1930 the CRC also summarily declined an invitation to participate in church-union discussions with five other Reformed and Presbyterian churches because Liberalism had already influenced and was tolerated in at least one of the cooperating churches. The Fundamentalist-modernist division within the ranks of American Protestantism increasingly shaped the thought and attitudes of the CRC. Liberalism was equated with heresy; opposition to it was often naively and uncritically confused with orthodoxy. Opposition to Liberalism became such a pronounced element in the CRC's consciousness that the mere identification of "liberal churches" in the membership of ecumenical organizations has come to preclude the possibility of CRC participation.

The special study committee reporting to the Synod of 1944 unequivocally and without precedent affirmed the catholicity of Christ's church. According to the report all Christian churches were related to one another and therefore were sisters, regardless of how deformed or defective they might be. The CRC inescapably has a calling with

112

respect to all Christ's churches. The committee, however, mixed catholic awareness with the conviction that Scripture allowed only one system of doctrine and one structure of government and discipline. To this awareness and conviction the committee added the opinion that of all Christ's churches the CRC was the closest historical approximation of the scriptural norms for church life. The only purpose and goal the report acknowledged and envisioned for interchurch relations was the eventual union of all churches. Consequently, the CRC's ecumenical task and calling was narrowly reduced to converting other churches to the Reformed faith and practice.

The report of 1944 addressed itself exclusively to official church correspondence and applied its genuinely catholic vision only to relationships between the CRC and other denominations. Somewhat surprisingly, the committee ignored the emerging ecumenical organizations of the time and apparently did not anticipate the possibility of the CRC meeting its catholic calling and responsibilities, even partially, through these agencies. In spite of this severe limitation, the report was nevertheless a historic landmark shaping the CRC's ecumenical and interchurch relations for over four decades. For its genuine catholic sensitivities, for its ecumenical scope and vision, and for its unqualified affirmation of responsibilities to other churches, it deserved to be a landmark. The report's respect for scriptural truth and Reformed confessional integrity is commendable. Its insistence that the CRC should not organically unite with another denomination, except on the basis of Scripture and in obedience to the Word of God, is correct. The committee's humble yet persistent claim, made without investigation, that of all the churches of Christ the CRC most closely approximated the scriptural norms for ecclesiastical life was more indicative of the committee's loyalty to the Reformed faith and the CRC than of the actual state of affairs in the CRC or, for that matter, in any other church. The statement and the atti-

tude of superiority that gave birth to it, however, showed
a lack of respect for the work of God's Word and Spirit in
other church communions. It also placed the CRC in the
enviable but impossible position in interchurch and ecumenical relations of having everything to teach and nothing to learn. As a consequence of this unfounded claim,
the CRC's ecumenical calling was narrowly reduced to
reproving and correcting other churches, an impossible
platform on which to build interchurch and ecumenical
relations. Unwittingly, the claim and attitude from which
it sprang only perpetuated the church's separation and
isolation. Seldom are such breadth of vision, narrowness
of purpose, and humble arrogance found in one report.

The committee failed to understand that there can be
different and equally valid perceptions of biblical truth. It
did not anticipate that through ecumenical dialogue God
might lead his church into a fuller understanding of the
truth than is represented in any one of the great church
traditions, including the Reformed.

Very naively, the committee assumed that if the
church's ecumenical vision was correct and its campaign
plan clearly understood, a method to implement the vision
and plan would naturally follow. But the committee never
presented the report it promised on just how to approach
other churches. It also failed to produce an ecumenical
method compatible with its theory and vision. When
prodded by the synod to complete the unfinished parts of
its mandate, the committee admitted extreme difficulty in
determining with certainty which churches were not only
historically Reformed but also Reformed in actual practice.
Eventually it resorted to the use of a letter of invitation to
official correspondence. In this way the committee shifted
from itself and the denomination the burden of responsibility for judging whether a church was really in fact Reformed and could in good conscience enter a relationship
of fellowship with the CRC, and placed it on the invited
churches. It is also noteworthy that the committee itself

114

soon reverted to the use of the old distinction between sister churches and churches in correspondence, in spite of its earlier criticism of the designation "sister church." While the committee emphatically affirmed, as a matter of scriptural principle, that all truly Reformed churches must unite as soon as possible, the committee itself never formulated a method for approaching and engaging other Reformed churches in union conversations. Neither did it identify a single Reformed denomination in America with which the CRC should unite. Nor did it ever draw up a plan or submit a proposal for reproving and correcting delinquent Reformed churches. Essential elements in the committee's plan and program were evidently incapable of implementation.

When the CRC struggled with the question of continuing membership in the National Association of Evangelicals, it became aware that it had no statement of biblical and ecumenical principles to guide it in matters pertaining to interchurch affiliation. To meet this need a special study committee was appointed in 1950. The committee was specifically asked to answer such fundamental questions as: (1) What are the nature, measure, and conditions of the church's ecumenical responsibility? (2) To what extent and in what manner may a confessional church unite in common witness with those who differ from its creeds? And (3) What are the implications of the unity of faith for interchurch fellowship and witness? Satisfactory answers to these basic questions must be found before a confessional church can formulate an ecumenical methodology and strategy. The committee did not do good work and left many of the questions unanswered.

The Synod of 1951 ignored the study committee's report and decided to sever its relationship with the NAE. No reasons were given for the decision. Not to give scriptural and confessional reasons for actions regarding membership in ecumenical organizations seems out of place for a Reformed church. The underlying problem was that the

CRC did not have a biblically and confessionally based statement of principles and strategy to guide it and to inform its decision. The letter that was sent to the officers of the NAE suggests that social factors loomed large in the decision to withdraw. The CRC was "closely knit" — socially cohesive and exclusivistic; the NAE was "loosely organized" — socially more inclusive. While these social differences may have been the most influential considerations, the CRC's distinctive Reformed confessional identity, which some in the church thought was threatened by continuing membership, probably played a role in the decision in spite of the NAE's and the CRC's mutual opposition to Liberalism.

The church-union conversations with the Reformed Presbyterian Church in North America (Covenanters) and with the Orthodox Presbyterian Church may have taught the CRC some lessons in interchurch relations. In these conversations the CRC met other confessional Reformed churches narrower in their standards of Reformed orthodoxy, more confident of their Reformed credentials, and more ready to reprove and correct than was the CRC. The insurmountable obstacles to union with the Covenanters were that church's practice of singing only psalms, without the accompaniment of musical instruments, and its refusal to allow church members to vote in civil elections or hold public office. For the CRC these were merely matters of practice and custom; for the Covenanters they were matters of scriptural principle. Pianos and organs within the church and the ballot box outside it appeared to stand in the way of obedience to the scriptural requirement of the unity of believers in Christ. The aborted effort indicates that even strict confessional Reformed churches can have quite different perceptions of biblical truth.

The conversations with the OPC began cautiously, proceeded deliberately, and deteriorated inexorably. The joint committee made slow but steady progress in resolving some real differences between the churches. Immediately after the synod and the general assembly authorized the joint committee to work toward the definite goal of organic union, the merger effort took a turn for the worse and from that point steadily declined. Once churches acquire separate and firmly fixed identities, they do not readily surrender them. When the general assembly appointed new representatives to the joint committee and asked them to investigate trends toward Liberalism in the CRC, the joint venture was over. The general assembly by its action unilaterally changed the committee's agenda. The CRC representatives to the conversations had been forced into an inferior status. Rather than tolerating the treatment and accepting correction and reproof, the CRC lost interest in a merger with the OPC. So the only serious attempt in the CRC to implement the scriptural principle stated in the 1944 report — that all churches Reformed in doctrine, government, and practice living in the same country must unite — ended in failure. Ecumenical and interchurch relationships by definition must be based on parity and mutual respect.

The special study committee appointed in 1966 to investigate the possibility of membership in the World Council of Churches did not have time to formulate principles and strategies for ecumenical relationships before facing the pressing and unavoidable question of whether or not membership in the WCC was permissible for a confessional Reformed church. On this question the committee divided.

Both the majority and minority attached themselves to different strands of thought deeply rooted in the Christian Reformed tradition. The majority picked up the separatist strand emphasizing the radical difference between faith and unbelief and the clear lines of demarcation separating the church from that which is not the church. The minority attached itself to the catholic strand within the tradition emphasizing the unity of believers in Christ and the CRC's calling and responsibility to all Christian churches. Both appealed to the report of 1944 to support their positions.

The decision of the Synod of 1924 to withdraw from the FCCC and the approach of the Committee on Ecumenicity and Church Correspondence to membership in the World Presbyterian Alliance were, however, more formative for the majority's position. The CRC withdrew from the FCCC because of the council's alleged Liberalism and the conviction of many within the denomination that all alliances between liberals and orthodox were contrary to the Word of God. The majority report on the World Council followed the structure of the earlier committee's report on the World Alliance, which found the alliance a theologically diverse and mixed company, including both orthodox and liberal churches. Given the variety of contemporary theologies, the committee judged that the alliance's constitution was too "dogmatically indistinct." Similarly, the majority found the WCC an inclusive organization, theologically diverse and mixed, that included "modernists." The WCC's Statement of Basis the majority likewise considered inadequate, given the theological differences present in the contemporary world. The majority also endorsed the earlier committee's opinion that "non-membership, when expressed in a Christian spirit and with a clear conscience, could be a more vocal and effective witness than joining a large ecumenical organization." The majority claimed that they were following the approach and methodology presented in the report of 1944. Yet they nowhere explained what precisely the approach or methodology of this report was. The committee in 1944 did not present a method or indicate how other churches should be approached. It candidly admitted that it did not know how to approach them and never submitted to the synod recommendations regarding methods to be followed in implementing the program it outlined in 1944.

The minority picked up the residual catholic, nonseparatist, and nonsectarian strand in the tradition. Understandably they endorsed the ecumenical vision of the 1944 report while scrupulously avoiding its narrow aims and offensive arrogance. Since the minority could not conscientiously argue for membership in the WCC, they failed to offer the synod a clear alternative on which it could act confidently and decisively. Lingering uncertainties regarding the nature of the WCC itself and the fact that the separatist element in the CRC's self-consciousness was still stronger than the ecumenical and catholic component made it impossible for the minority to recommend the only clear alternative, membership in the council.

The CRC has not reconsidered membership in the WCC. The catholicity and unity of Christ's church has not yet penetrated the CRC consciousness so as to create enough yearning for ecumenical involvement to implement the ecumenical vision either articulated in the report of 1944 or embodied in the WCC. The World Council, by the mere fact of its existence, is and continues to be a more eloquent witness to the catholicity of the church than the CRC's nonmembership in that body is to the truth of the gospel. This is so not because truth is unimportant in ecumenical relationships or because the CRC is unfaithful to the truth of Scripture as it perceives it, but because nonmembership is a nonverbal form of witness and inevitably is susceptible to a variety of interpretations, including the sectarian possibility of separation for no other reason than to be separate.

The CRC has established and maintained interchurch relations only with strict confessional Reformed churches. It did so first by a system of official correspondence and later by use of the designation "churches in ecclesiastical fellowship." The CRC is also a charter member of two confessional Reformed ecumenical bodies, the Reformed Ecumenical Council (formerly the Reformed Ecumenical Synod) and the North American Presbyterian and Reformed Council (NAPARC). In all these interchurch and ecumenical endeavors, the CRC has either unilaterally or in cooperation with other equally confessional Reformed churches set the terms for affiliation and fellowship.

For reasons peculiar to itself, the CRC has not been able to establish and maintain relations with Christian churches other than confessional Reformed ones. The difficulty is in no small measure due to the fact that in the past it was unable to develop an ecumenical approach and methodology compatible with its ecumenical vision and sense of calling. In the absence of a carefully worked out method to implement its catholic vision and ecumenical calling, the CRC has attempted to apply its traditional, internal standards for church fellowship to relationships with other churches and ecumenical organizations. In the past it has not recognized that there can be varying degrees of intimacy in church and interchurch fellowship, and consequently that different standards of purity in doctrine and discipline can legitimately be accepted as conditions of ecumenical and interchurch affiliation. In other words, the CRC has not accepted as a working principle the fact that churches in a close-knit denominational fellowship and those entering an organic union must be united in doctrine and discipline in closer bonds of fellowship than is required of churches in loosely knit, more inclusive ecumenical organizations. CRC synods have never addressed these issues, except in the context of specific recommendations and debates regarding membership in interdenominational and ecumenical organizations. Consequently, the church has simply used the standards for orthodoxy and discipline that regulate its own denominational life and applied them to other ecumenical bodies and their member churches. Understandably, the church's ecumenical involvement has not extended beyond the narrow limits of Reformed confessional orthodoxy.

The new Ecumenical Charter has broken some new ground that may enable the church to fulfill its ecumenical task more confidently and effectively. Perhaps most noteworthy is the recognition that churches — including the CRC — have different perceptions of biblical truth that can be shared with one another, and that they can trust God to lead his church into a fuller understanding of that truth. This insight may relieve the CRC of its historic sense of superiority in understanding and purity and may make it teachable in the ecumenical arena. The charter's endorsement of dialogue as a legitimate means to engage in ecumenical conversation may also provide a basis and framework for a feasible approach and working method for implementing its ecumenical calling.

Unlike the report of 1944, the charter encourages the CRC to pursue its ecumenical calling through ecumenical organizations. If the church is sincere in recommending this approach, it will no longer be able unilaterally to set the terms and conditions for all its ecumenical relationships but will have to find ways and means, perhaps even rationales, to fit into existing organizations consistent with the demands of its own confessional integrity.

The CRC has long feared that membership in ecumenical organizations is a potential threat to its separate existence and to its distinctive confessional Reformed character. Two statements in the new charter, reflecting insights learned from modern ecumenicity, speak to these concerns and may offer some relief. The charter humbly recognizes that the precise form of the unity being sought for Christ's church remains unknown. The charter also realistically affirms the propriety of diversity within unity, a diversity that includes differences in confessional formulas, church order, and worship.

To date, the new charter, with its biblical and ecumenical principles and methodology, has not penetrated the consciousness of the CRC or significantly influenced its ecumenical outreach. The real test will come when the church acts on specific recommendations for membership in ecumenical organizations. If the CRC continues to apply to ecumenical organizations corporately and to their member churches individually the same standards for faith and discipline that regulate its own denominational life, its ecumenical involvement will not extend beyond the narrowly delimited boundaries of strict confessional orthodoxy, and its biblically and confessionally imposed catholic Christian calling and responsibility will remain unfulfilled. For the CRC to meet its as yet unfulfilled ecumenical calling and responsibility, it will have to realistically recognize that different kinds of ecumenical organizations require different degrees of intimacy in fellowship from their member bodies.

At present the CRC is not ecumenically well situated. It remains isolated from mainline American Protestantism and from the world church. Relations with the Reformed Churches in the Netherlands (GKN) have deteriorated, with little prospect of improvement in the near future. Relations with the Reformed Church in South Africa (RCSA) are in jeopardy and appear on the verge of curtailment. The Reformed Ecumenical Council (REC) remains in a serious state of crisis. The basic problems that created the crisis remain unresolved, and with the two largest member churches — the GKN and the Dutch Reformed Church in South Africa (DRC) — finding it difficult to muster solid majority support within their own ranks for continuing membership, the future of that organization is uncertain. NAPARC is the brightest spot on the CRC's ecumenical horizon, but this small coterie of churches represents only an exceedingly small portion of Christ's church.

The Reformed Church in America (RCA) never accepted without qualification the CRC's unilateral terms and conditions for fellowship. In spite of this the CRC has maintained a relationship with the RCA. Similarities in history and confession and the close geographical proximity of many of the congregations of the two denominations have made ignoring the RCA impossible. Interdenominational unity and cooperation that respect the separate existence of each denomination appear to be allowing the churches to express their unity on an interim basis while continuing to engage in dialogue. For a union of the churches to take place, the RCA's Reformed consciousness and sense of identity will have to become clearer and more sharply focused, and the CRC's catholic consciousness and sense of identity will have to broaden and deepen.

Since the CRC became a member of the NAE in 1988, it may reasonably be presumed that the NAE now meets the denomination's standards for Christian orthodoxy and fellowship. Membership in the NAE is not a present or potential threat to the CRC's separate existence. Consistent with the ecclesiastical independentism of most American evangelicals, the NAE in its Statement of Faith obligates members to confess no more regarding the church than the spiritual unity of believers. This confession falls far short of the catholicity taught in Scripture and confessed in the ancient creeds and Reformed confessions. In the unanimous opinion of the delegates to the Synod of 1988, membership in the NAE does not pose a present threat to the confessional Reformed character of the CRC. Whether it represents a potential and long-term danger remains to be seen.

The CRC's roots in the Dutch Reformed tradition are getting shallower all the time. It can no longer look to the GKN for leadership and assistance in preserving and developing its distinctive Reformed tradition. Unless the CRC establishes relationships with historically Reformed bodies in America adequate to counterbalance the potentially formative influences of American evangelicalism, the church may more and more experience difficulty in maintaining its confessional Reformed character.

During the twentieth-century ecumenical age, the CRC has remained faithful to the truth as it perceives it. The authority of God's Word has been respected and esteemed at a time when in many churches the Bible's authority has been undermined. Ironically, the clear testimony of Scripture and the creeds to the catholicity of the church has made little impact on the CRC, and the church for the most part remains unaware of the fact that loyalty to the truth includes commitment to the ecumenical dimensions of the Christian faith. The catholic vision and ecumenical calling articulated in the report of 1944 and the Ecumenical Charter of 1987 have not yet permeated the heart and mind of the church. Its catholic Christian consciousness and sense of identity remain immature and underdeveloped. Scripture alone has not yet aroused the church sufficiently to bring about a fundamental change. The American environment, the most ecclesiastically diverse of any nation in the world, also does not contribute to catholic maturity. If and when the cultural situation changes, producing sharper lines of separation between faith and unbelief and between the church and the world, on the one hand, and producing a greater awareness of oneness in Christ and the need to manifest that oneness visibly, on the other, there may then be a resurgence of catholic Christian consciousness in the CRC.

Index

10-11, 110-11; union conversations with, 13-15, 24; union with, 2-4

Reformed Church in Japan, 41

Reformed Church in the U.S. (German Reformed), 24

Reformed Churches in the Netherlands (GKN): deteriorating relations with, 87-92, 123; interchurch relations with, 13, 26-29, 42, 52; membership in RES, 79-81, 84, 122; membership in WCC, 61-62, 65, 77-78

Reformed Church in South Africa (RCSA): deteriorating relations with, 92-95, 123; interchurch relations with, 16, 20, 26, 28-29, 42

Reformed Ecumenical Synod (RES): 57, 59, 62, 65, 70, 73, 107; apartheid and racial issues, 81-84; establishment of, 26-29, 112; GKN membership in, 79-81

Reformed Presbyterian Church (Evangelical Synod), 85, 87

Reformed Presbyterian Church in North America (Covenanters): interchurch relations with, 18, 41, 85; union conversations with, 51-52, 116

Remonstrant Brotherhood in the Netherlands, 109

Report of 1944: 30-43; application to ecumenical organizations, 47-48, 52, 57, 59-60, 65, 71, 73, 75, 107, 123; comparison with Ecumenical Charter, 99-102, 121; evaluation of, 112-15, 117-19

Roman Catholic Church, 36-37, 56, 75

Rutgers, William, 42

Schippers, C., 92

Sister churches: meaning of, 30-34, 43, 88-89; names of, 16, 20, 60

Southern Baptists, 75

Speer, Robert E., 23

Status confessionis, 82-83

Stek, John, 92

Snyman, W. J., 28

Timmerman, John, 22-23

Toit, du S., 28

True Reformed Dutch Church, 11-12

United Church of Canada, 109

United Church of Christ, 109

United Presbyterian Church of North America (UPC), 12-13, 18, 24, 41

United Presbyterian Church in the U.S.A., 60, 86, 109. *See also Presbyterian Church* in the U.S.A.

Vande Luister, J., 4, 6

Van Dellen, I., 28

Vanden Bosch, Koene, 6, 8, 10